# GOSPEL FOUNDATIONS

## A WANDERING PEOPLE

### VOL. 2 | Exodus–Judges

2

From the creators of *The Gospel Project*, *Gospel Foundations* is a six-volume resource that teaches the storyline of Scripture. It is comprehensive in scope yet concise enough to be completed in just one year. Each seven-session volume includes videos to help your group understand the way each text fits into the storyline of the Bible.

ISBN 9781535915533 • Item 005805887

Dewey decimal classification: 230

Subject headings: CHRISTIANITY / GOSPEL / SALVATION

EDITORIAL TEAM

Ben Trueblood
*Director, Student Ministry*

JohnPaul Basham
*Manager, Student Ministry Publishing*

Andy McLean
*Content Editor*

Grace Pepper
*Production Editor*

Alli Quattlebaum
*Graphic Designer*

We believe that the Bible has God for its author; salvation for its end; and truth, without any mixture of error, for its matter and that all Scripture is totally true and trustworthy. To review LifeWay's doctrinal guideline, please visit lifeway.com/doctrinalguideline.

To order additional copies of this resource, write to LifeWay Resources Customer Service; One LifeWay Plaza; Nashville, TN 37234; fax 615-251-5933; call toll free 800-458-2772; order online at LifeWay.com; email orderentry@lifeway.com; or visit the LifeWay Christian Store serving you.

Printed in the United States of America

Student Ministry Publishing
LifeWay Resources
One LifeWay Plaza
Nashville, TN 37234

# CONTENTS

# ABOUT *THE GOSPEL PROJECT*

*Gospel Foundations* is from the creators of *The Gospel Project*, which exists to point kids, students, and adults to the gospel of Jesus Christ through weekly group Bible studies and additional resources that show how God's plan of redemption unfolds throughout Scripture and still today, compelling them to join the mission of God.

*The Gospel Project* provides theological yet practical, age-appropriate Bible studies that immerse your entire church in the story of the gospel, helping to develop a gospel culture that leads to gospel mission:

## Gospel Story

Immersing people of all ages in the storyline of Scripture: God's plan to rescue and redeem His creation through His Son, Jesus Christ.

## Gospel Culture

Inspiring communities where the gospel saturates our experience and doubters become believers who become declarers of the gospel.

## Gospel Mission

Empowering believers to live on mission, declaring the good news of the gospel in word and deed.

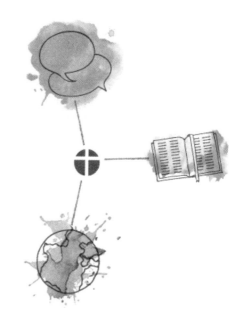

# HOW TO USE THIS STUDY

This Bible-study book includes seven weeks of content for group and personal study. Each session is divided into the following components:

## Introduction

Every session contains an intro option for your group time. allowing there to be a natural transition into the material for that week.

## Setting the Context

This section is designed to provide the context to the biblical passage being discussed. It will help group members to not only better understand the passage under consideration for each session, but also how the biblical storyline connects between each session. It is also in this section that you will find the reference to the informational graphic for each session, once again helping students to have a deeper understanding into the storyline of Scripture.

## Session Videos

Each session has a corresponding video to help tell the Bible story. After watching the video, spend some time discussing the questions provided, as well any additional questions raised by your students in response to the video.

## Group Discussion

After watching the video, continue the group discussion by reading the Scripture passages and discussing the questions on these pages. Additional content is also provided on these pages to grant additional clarity into the meaning of these passages. In addition, it is in this section that you find the Christ Connection, showing students how all of Scripture points to Jesus.

## Head, Heart, Hands

This section is designed to close out your group time by personally reflecting on how God's Story challenges the way we think, feel, and live as a result. Because God's Word is capable of changing everything about a person, this section seeks to spell out how each session is able to transform our Heads, Hearts, and Hands.

## Personal Study

Five personal devotions are provided for each session to take individuals deeper into Scripture and to supplement the content introduced in the group study. With biblical teaching and introspective questions, these sections challenge individuals to grow in their understanding of God's Word and to respond in faith.

# GOD'S WORD TO YOU

*A LIFE WORTH DYING FOR*

In the beginning, God created all things good. With the making of humankind as male and female, He even declared His creation to be very good. Paradise was the location; abundant life was the experience, that is, until the taint of sin covered the world through the rebellion of Adam and Eve against their Creator.

As a result, humanity lost its paradise and was separated from the God who created all things good. Death was God's warning for disobedience, and death became the reality—the death of living apart from God (sin), the death of life (physical death), and the death of eternal separation from God's goodness (spiritual death).

But the God of all good things was not finished. He called a people to Himself to be a light to the world. He gave them His holy expectations that they should follow. He made provision for sin through sacrifices. And even when His people continued to rebel against Him, He promised life from death.

In comes Jesus, the Son of God sent into the world to make all things new— "In him was life, and that life was the light of men" (John 1:4). "Full of grace and truth," Jesus obeyed all of the Father's holy expectations (1:14). He is the "Lamb of God, who takes away the sin of the world!" (1:29). He laid down His life on a cross to secure life for those who follow Him (10:11), and He proved it in His resurrection when He took up His life again (10:18). A thief comes to steal, kill, and destroy; Jesus came so we might once again have life and have it in abundance (10:10).

So how should we respond to this good news? By turning from sin (repentance) and believing in Jesus (faith). "The one who loves his life will lose it, and the one who hates his life in this world will keep it for eternal life" (12:25). The riches and pleasures of this world cannot compare to the eternal life found in Jesus.

# GOD HEARS HIS PEOPLE

*GOD SEES THE SUFFERING OF THE OPPRESSED
AND PROMISES REDEMPTION.*

# INTRODUCTION

In the 1980's a song called "Walk Like an Egyptian" by the Bangles shot up the charts and led to people of all ages doing the light-hearted "sand dance." In the side profile position, with arms extended, elbows and wrists bent at right angles, with one arm up and one arm down and alternate knees lifting and bending at right angles, the dancers walked while moving their heads forward and backward in rhythmic fashion. (The move was supposed to reflect ancient Egyptian art.) Even today, people unfamiliar with the song know the dance.

"Walk Like an Egyptian" doesn't lead you to take Egypt very seriously. For many in the West, Egypt is known primarily for its ancient pyramids and King Tut's tomb. In the period of the Exodus, however, people feared Egypt. Egypt had mighty pharaohs, great building projects, and, some believe, dark powers. Everyone took Egypt seriously. Israel certainly wasn't doing the Egyptian sand dance—they were enslaved to the Egyptians. And it's the injustice of their slavery that sets the backdrop for God's glorious deliverance.

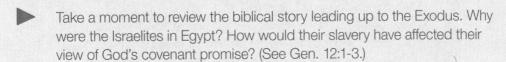 Take a moment to review the biblical story leading up to the Exodus. Why were the Israelites in Egypt? How would their slavery have affected their view of God's covenant promise? (See Gen. 12:1-3.)

# SETTING THE CONTEXT

God's chosen people, the bearers of His covenant with Abraham, lived in Egypt for four hundred years as slaves. Because the population continued to multiply, Pharaoh ordered every male baby of Israelite birth be thrown into the Nile. One Israelite mother hid her son in her home as long as she could. When she could no longer do so, she put him in a basket and floated him down the Nile in faith that somehow he would be saved.

As God would have it, Pharaoh's own daughter found the basket and named the boy Moses. He lived as her son in the palace until one day he sought to defend his people. He killed an Egyptian taskmaster, then ran for his life into the land of Midian, where he lived as a shepherd for forty years, not knowing that he would play a crucial role in God's plan of deliverance. "Moses' Life" (p. 10) provides a quick overview of Moses' part in God's plan.

# MOSES' *LIFE*

| | |
|---|---|
| **BIRTH–40** | **A Son In Egypt**<br>• Born, placed in a basket in the Nile River, found by Pharaoh's daughter (Ex. 2)<br>• Killed an Egyptian taskmaster beating a Hebrew slave (see Ex 2; Acts 7:23-24)<br>• Fled to Midian (Ex. 2) |
| **40–80** | **A Shepherd in Midian**<br>• Married Zipporah and had a family (Ex. 2)<br>• Met with Yahweh at the burning bush (Ex. 3-4; cf. Acts 7:30) |
| **80–120** | **A Prophet for God**<br>• Returned to Egypt to confront Pharaoh with the plagues (Ex. 4–12)<br>• Led the Israelites in the exodus and in crossing the Red Sea (Ex. 12–14)<br>• Led the Israelites to Mount Sinai (Ex. 15–19)<br>• Gave the people God's law and His instructions (Ex. 20–Num. 10)<br>• Led the Israelites to southern edge of the promised land (Num. 10)<br>  – The people rebelled; condemned to wilderness for 40 years (Num. 13–14)<br>• Disobeyed God in how he brought forth water from a rock (Num. 20)<br>• After 40 years, led the Israelites to eastern edge of promised land (Num. 22)<br>• Allowed to see the promised land but not enter it (Deut. 3)<br>• Died on Mount Nebo (Deut. 34) |

# SESSION VIDEOS

Watch this session's video, and then continue the group
discussion using the following guide.

▶ What ideas or phrases stood out to you most in the video? Why?

▶ In what ways are we, or have we been, like the people of Israel, enslaved
and in bondage?

# GROUP DISCUSSION

As a group, read Exodus 3:2-10.

★ What is evident about the character of God from these verses?

▶ Why do you think God reminded Moses that He is the God of his ancestors?

▶ How do you think you would have responded had you been Moses?

In this passage, we read of the burning bush and the angel of the Lord who appeared to Moses. God spoke to Moses and called him to remove his sandals as an act of reverence. God then identified Himself with the patriarchs, Abraham, Isaac, and Jacob (3:6). Before God entered a relationship with Moses, He entered a relationship with Moses' fathers (see 2:24). God was also giving Moses a bit of personal history of Himself.

All of this was to show Moses that the God of the burning bush wasn't an unknown God; He was the God who acted on behalf of these men earlier in history. Notice that God does not say, "I was the God of Abraham, Isaac, and Jacob..." but rather, "I am the God of Abraham, Isaac, and Jacob..." This indicates that God's people never really die; but remain in eternal relationship with God.

Though four hundred years had passed, God had not forgotten His promise to His people. He remained the same God who called Abraham, and it was time for Him to intervene on behalf of His people. At times, we might be tempted to doubt or forget the promises of God, but we can know for certain that God has not forgotten about us.

# GROUP DISCUSSION *CONT.*

**As a group, read Exodus 3:11-15.**

▶ When have you felt like Moses, unqualified to do what you know God has called you to do?

★ How might God's answers to Moses encourage you when you feel unqualified?

▶ What is significant about God's revelation of His name?

Moses wasn't eager to go on this mission. In his dialogue with God, Moses made several excuses for not obeying God's call. But God responded to each of Moses' excuses and questions with statements about His own sovereignty and power.

Moses' first argument was about himself: "Who am I?" (3:11), he asked. He felt insufficient. He essentially asked, "Have you considered my resume? For the last forty years, I've been in a wilderness." Stop and think about it. Even though he was once a prince, Moses was now a humble shepherd. God asked this shepherd to confront the most powerful person in the world and tell him to let his slaves go free. This would be sort of like an average blue-collar worker declaring war on a president of a major country. Can you imagine your plumber declaring war on Russia?

Moses was an average guy, and alone he didn't have great influence. Yet God responded to Moses by revealing what was most important: Himself. God said, "I will certainly be with you" (3:12a). Throughout the Bible, this is what God's leaders need in order to lead: God's presence. It's the non-negotiable for serving God. Think about Joseph, Moses, Joshua, Gideon, Jehoshaphat, and the disciples. (See Matt. 28:18-20.) God was with them all.

**As a group, read Exodus 7:14-18.**

▶ These verses contain just one of several signs God gave through Moses. Why do you think God chose to deliver His people using signs like these?

⭐ What would these signs have demonstrated both to God's people and the Egyptians?

▶ Should we as God's people still expect signs like these? Why or why not?

In performing these signs and wonders, God demonstrated His power over all false gods. Each one of the signs He performed targeted a particular god that the Egyptians worshiped. In this case, the Egyptians worshiped the Nile, and God showed His power over that god by turning the river to blood. Ultimately, the greatest sign and wonder God performed was raising Jesus from the dead, proving that Jesus is Lord even over death.

CHRIST CONNECTION

*God told Moses His name "I AM" as a revelation of His transcendent self-existence. Jesus is the eternal Son of God, the great "I AM," who came to save us from sin.*

# OUR MISSION

**Head**

What are some ways we can increase our sense of reverence for God?

What is the difference between being "terrified" by God and being "awed" by God?

**Heart**

How is it that sin causes us to turn our hearts from God and His Word?

What are some ways we can guard our hearts from being hardened by the deceitfulness of sin?

**Hands**

When have you, like Moses, felt that God was asking you to do something you couldn't do?

How can resting in God's promises and trusting His sovereignty help you be obedient to Him?

# PERSONAL STUDY: DAY 1

⭐ **The point: God responds by listening to the prayers of the oppressed.**

▶ Read Exodus 2:23–3:10.

Note the action of the Israelites that prompted God to respond (3:7). What was God's response (3:8)?

In your Bible, underline the ways God took notice of what was happening to the Israelites in Exodus 3:7-9. Make a list of what God saw, heard, and knew.

| Saw | Heard | Knew |
|-----|-------|------|
|     |       |      |

Summarize God's plan to rescue His people. Why do you think God revealed Himself to Moses (3:6)?

Moses was part of God's response to the cries of the Israelites. He was God's choice for leading the people out of the oppression of the Egyptians. God not only heard and listened, but also took action.

▶ Respond

God always listens. When you cry out to God, He responds. In times of struggle are you quick to turn to Christ or do you tend to turn to your family, friends, or something else?

It is easy to complain and focus on our trials, forgetting to cry out to God—the only One who can bring hope and change to any situation we face. Reflect on a time when God responded to your cry. Ask yourself: *Did this draw me closer in relationship with Him?*

## ⭐ The point: God responds by revealing His character.

▶ **Read Exodus 3:11-15.**

What qualified Moses to become the one who would lead the Israelites out of Egypt? Explain.

God's presence was a game-changer. Moses felt intimidated and incapable of standing before Pharaoh, so he questioned God. List the questions Moses raised about his own ability to complete the task God gave to him.

Every time Moses questioned, God answered by giving His credentials. Underline in your Bible the titles that God used to describe Himself in verses 14-15.

What do those titles, and God's resposes to Moses, reveal about His character? Explain.

▶ **Respond**

Like Moses, we may feel unqualified for the job God has called us to do. Consider your own life and journal your response to the following questions.

- Has God called you to do something that you refused or brushed off because you were afraid? Explain.
- Have you questioned what He asked you to do, wondering if you were up to the task? Explain.
- What do you think God wants you to do now? What are some things that might hold you back from accomplishing this? What would encourage you to go for it?

Ask God to give you the courage to trust in His promises and act on His calling for your life.

# PERSONAL STUDY: DAY 3

⭐ ## The point: God responds by promising redemption.

Consider the word *misery.* List a few things that come to mind when you hear this word.

Now, consider the word *favor.* List a few things that come to mind when you hear this word.

▶ **Read Exodus 3:16-22.**

God spoke clearly as He laid out His plan for Moses. Summarize the main theme of the message God asked Moses to give to His people.

In verse 20, underline the phrase "stretch out my hand." What do you think this means? What did God say would happen when He stretched out His hand?

God's touch was powerful. When He acted, there was always a response. His power never failed. Besides their release from the Egyptians, what did God tell the Israelites He would give them?

▶ **Respond**

Does knowing the depth of the power of God increase your confidence that He will act on your behalf?

Is there something you need to ask God to give you clear direction and reassurance about? Pray and ask Him to help you clearly see what He wants you to do.

Take a moment to remember that the God who rescued the Israelites is the same God who lives in you.

# PERSONAL STUDY: DAY 4

✪ **The point: God reveals His glory by comforting His people.**

▶ Read Exodus 6:2-9.

List all the promises God made to the Israelites in this passage. Which ones do you think were the most meaningful to the people? Why?

Promises give hope, and God's promises are always true. He never breaks them. Since God is truthful and always keeps His promises, we can trust His Words. We have hope as He comforts us.

In verse 5, God said He "heard" and "remembered." He acknowledged that He heard His people when they cried out to Him, He saw their pain, and He remembered the promises He made to them. He constantly reassured the Israelites when He spoke. What do you think this reassurance did for their trust in Him? How do you think His words comforted His people?

Even in the darkest times, God is our hope. His promises make us hopeful for what lies ahead and they remind us of His glory—that He can do what He says He will do.

How do God's promises to the Israelites reveal His glory?

▶ Respond

God made significant promises to the Israelites, but because of their circumstances, they still had trouble believing. Think of a time in your journey with Christ when your circumstances made it difficult to trust God's promises.

Is there a particular promise from God's Word that gives you confidence, comfort, or peace? Jot it down in a place where you can read it each day.

# PERSONAL STUDY: DAY 5

⭐ **The point: God reveals His glory by confronting false gods.**

▶ Read Exodus 7:14-25.

According to verse 14, what was the reason Pharaoh refused to let the Israelites leave?


Pharaoh did not listen because He did not fear or acknowledge God. His heart was hardened. Because of this, God set events into motion that made it impossible for anyone to ignore His glory, power, or His request for His people's freedom.

What was the first plague God sent (vv. 19-20)? Explain.


The Egyptians worshiped the Nile, and it had various gods associated with it. By striking the river with the first plague, a loud statement was being made. God showed Himself to be more powerful that any Egyptian deity. The Nile was the heartbeat of the people, and God had taken their confidence with one strike from Aaron's rod.

By turning this river to blood, God was not only carrying out judgment on the Egyptians, but also on their gods. Why do you think God did this? What might these other "gods" look like today?


How did Pharaoh respond to God's confrontation of the false gods (vv. 22-23)? Why is this important?


▶ Respond

Do you think Moses and Aaron were afraid as they stood before Pharaoh? They stood before the most powerful man on earth because God sent them with His message. Have you ever had to do something that required standing up to someone powerful or important on behalf of God (or God's message)?

The Bible never indicates the men were not afraid, but ultimately their faith was stronger than their fear. What steps do you need to take for your faith to become stronger than your fear in following God? List a few ideas in the margin of your Bible beside today's passage.

# GOD DELIVERS
# HIS PEOPLE

*EVEN IN HIS JUDGMENT, GOD OFFERS SALVATION
THROUGH THE SACRIFICE OF A SUBSTITUTE.*

# INTRODUCTION

God had not forgotten His people or His promise to them. He revealed Himself to Moses and sent him as His representative to confront Pharaoh and all the false gods of the Egyptians. In doing so, God would rescue His people, but He would rescue them in a way that highlighted His great power and glory.

Why is it important for us to note that God rescued His people in a way that brought Him glory?

The deliverance had begun, but the hardhearted Pharaoh was not ready to let the people of God go and worship Him. Time and time again, Pharaoh promised to let Israel go, only to go back on his promise and keep them in captivity. And each time, God brought more judgment on the land. As the conflict rose to a crescendo, God would perform one final wonder that would not only secure the release of His people but would be a powerful indicator of the greater deliverance to come in Christ.

 Have you ever participated in or learned about the Passover meal? If so, what was your experience like?

# SETTING THE CONTEXT

"Let My people go!" This was the message God tasked Moses to deliver to Pharaoh. Along with that message, God promised Moses that He would bring about great acts of judgment upon the land of Egypt.

Despite the severity of these events, God always spared His people. There was no darkness in their land, no hail fell on the Israelites, and none of their livestock died. Yet Pharaoh was unwilling to recognize the authority God had over him. Even after all the devastation on the land, there was one more judgment coming from God. This judgment would be so severe that Pharaoh would finally relent and God's people would go free. But this plague was also different from the ones before in that a Passover lamb was required for the Israelites to be spared. "Seeing Jesus in the Exodus" (p. 22) shows how this Passover lamb foreshadows Jesus Christ.

## SEEING
# JESUS *IN THE* EXODUS

| OLD TESTAMENT | NEW TESTAMENT |
|---|---|
| **Yahweh, The LORD**<br>"I AM" (Ex. 3:14-15) | **Jesus**<br>"I AM" (John 8:58) |
| **Moses**<br>A Mediator (Ex. 32:11-14) | **Jesus**<br>The One Mediator (1 Tim. 2:5-6) |
| **Moses**<br>A Prophet (Deut. 18:18-19) | **Jesus**<br>The Prophet (Acts 3:22-26) |
| **Israel, God's Firstborn Son**<br>Called Out of Egypt (Ex. 4:22-23) | **Israel, God's Firstborn Son**<br>The Fulfillment (Matt. 2:15) |
| **The Passover Lamb**<br>Protection from the Plagues (Ex. 12) | **Christ, Our Passover**<br>Protection from Sin (1 Cor. 5:7-8) |

# SESSION VIDEOS

Watch this session's video, and then continue the group discussion using the following guide.

▶ What ideas or phrases stood out to you most in the video? Why?

▶ What are some specific ways the Passover foreshadows the death of Jesus Christ centuries later?

# GROUP DISCUSSION

As a group, read Exodus 12:3-8, 12-13.

▶ What was the distinguishing characteristic that would keep God's people safe from the final plague?

▶ Why is that an important detail for us to remember as Christians?

⭐ What are some things we might be trusting in other than God to keep us safe?

Verses 6-7 tell us the fate of the unblemished lamb—it was to be killed at twilight. The slain lamb would be a vivid reminder to everyone that all deserve judgment. (See Rom. 3:23.) Consequently, a blameless life had to be sacrificed in the place of the guilty people who needed salvation. The blood of the lamb was to be applied to the Israelites doorposts (v. 7). The obedience of placing the blood on their doorposts showed that they believed God would keep His word and pass over, sparing that house from judgment. So, Israel escaped judgment through this sacrifice, and salvation was accomplished by faith in the work of the substitute. The blood on their doors served as a sign that judgment had already fallen at that house. Just as the plagues were a sign to Egypt of God's justice and judgment, now the Passover was a sign of God's mercy to Israel.

Thus, we see God continue to keep the promise of Genesis 3:15 and the Abrahamic covenant. In the midst of looming judgment, God provided. He protected Israel from slavery and death for future salvation. In accomplishing this, He said, "When I see the blood, I will pass over you. No plague will be among you to destroy you when I strike the land of Egypt." God accepted the blood of the sacrifice and passed over their sin.

▶ The blood on the door was a public statement for all to see. How does this influence the way we think of our Christian faith? What characteristics should distinguish your life from the lives of others?

# GROUP DISCUSSION *CONT.*

Through the end of chapter 14, we find one of the most important stories in the Bible: the crossing of the Red Sea. God will get His people out of Egypt through the miracle of parting the sea, and He will judge the Egyptians by swallowing them up in the sea.

**As a group, read Exodus 12:29-32.**

⭐ How do these verses reveal the severity of sin?

▶ What similarities do you see between the world of the Egyptians and the world of today when it comes to God's judgment?

▶ How should the severity of God's judgment and the magnitude of His mercy affect the way we live?

In this passage, we see God's redeeming power displayed in a "great reversal." God began by striking down the firstborns of Egypt and ended the debates with one cataclysmic sign. He judged all of Egypt without distinction, from rich to poor, good to bad. The cries in the land extended to all peoples. The destroyer went through the mightiest nation in the world, like a knife through butter.

Through the tenth plague, God turned evil on its head. Pharaoh had enacted an unrighteous judgment on Hebrew boys by throwing them into the Nile. Now, God enacted a righteous judgment on the Egyptians. Pharaoh's judgment came back on his head. In addition, by striking down the "gods" of Egypt, particularly Pharaoh's son, God shows Pharaoh that he isn't God, and neither is his son. There's only one true God! This blow hurts Egypt not only personally through the loss of the son of succession—but also theologically as God's power over their gods is displayed.

**As a group, read Exodus 14:13-28.**

▶ Does it surprise you that the Israelites were so afraid, given what they had already witnessed? Why or why not?

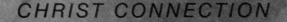 In what ways are we like the Israelites in this manner?

Moses obeyed the instructions God gave him (v. 21). But consider the situation and God's instructions: Pharaoh was coming, the people were complaining, and God essentially said, "Hold out your stick, and I will part the waters!" Why? Once again the theme of God's glory is repeated: "I will get glory over Pharaoh" (14:17-18). It may have sounded foolish, but Moses obeyed.

As the Egyptians pursued the Israelites, "the Lord looked down," majestically exalted above all (v. 24). He threw the Egyptians into a panic and clogged the wheels of their fine chariots (vv. 24-25). They should have fled, but they didn't. After Israel crossed the sea, Moses stretched out his staff so that the waters came down on the Egyptians and everything with them (v. 26). This was total elimination. At daybreak, the Israelites could see God's victory, for the Egyptians were swallowed up when the water went back into the gap (vv. 27-28).

## CHRIST CONNECTION

*Just as a spotless lamb was sacrificed to spare God's people from His judgment in Egypt, so also Jesus Christ is the Passover Lamb who was sacrificed to protect us from God's judgment of sin.*

# OUR MISSION

## ⭕ Head

Why is it sometimes difficult to trust God's guidance? What are some things we learn as we walk by faith in God's guidance?

How do we give glory to God by obeying His instructions even when we don't understand His purpose?

## ♥ Heart

What is the connection between our worship of the Lamb, Jesus, and our witness to the gospel?

Share of a time when you responded in obedience as a result of God's goodness in your life.

## ✋ Hands

Do you find it difficult to talk about the coming judgment of God? If so, why?

What difference does it make in talking about judgment knowing that Jesus bears the wrath of judgment in our place through faith in Him?

# PERSONAL STUDY: DAY 1

## ⭐ The point: God warns us of impending judgment.

▶ **Read Genesis 1:1; review Exodus 11:1-3.**

What did God tell Moses would happen to Pharaoh? How did God say Pharaoh would react?

▶ **Read Exodus 11:4-8.**

Think through the following: Moses told Pharaoh God would go throughout Egypt around midnight. Describe what would happen when God went throughout the land.

Compare and contrast what would happen to the Egyptians and Israelites.

| Egyptians | Israelites |
|---|---|
| | |

God sent multiple plagues to offer Pharaoh a chance to obey, but Pharaoh ignored them all. The consequence for Pharaoh's sin would be death.

In the same way, our sin has consequences. Read Romans 6:23 and fill in the blanks.

The consequence for sin is _____, but the

gift of God is _____  _____ .

God gives believers eternal life with Him instead of what we deserve, which is eternal separation.

▶ **Respond**

There was a "great cry" in Egypt when death struck. Sin leads to death. Believers are alive in Christ, but those who don't know Him are dead in their sin (Eph. 2:1-3). God warned us through His Word, and we are called to tell others. How does this affect your thoughts about sharing the gospel? Journal your response.

⭐ **The point: God offers protection through a perfect sacrifice.**

▶ **Read Exodus 12:1-13.**

The Passover was so important God changed the Israelites' calendar so this would always be the first month of their year. What does this tell you about the importance of the instructions outlined in today's passage?

Describe the instructions given for the animal sacrifice.

According to Deuteronomy 17:1, why was it so important to follow the directions given in verse 5?

Why did the Israelites have to mark their doorposts with blood (vv. 7,13)?

God offered the Israelites His protection through the blood of an unblemished lamb. His judgment of death passed over the houses marked by the blood of the lamb. Today, believers no longer participate in animal sacrifices because Jesus, the Lamb of God, was the final, perfect sacrifice for sin. His blood covers us from the judgment of spiritual death.

▶ **Respond**

How does it affect you to know you deserve death because of your sin?

Jesus paid the price for you, and all of God's judgment was taken out on Him on the cross. How does this cause you to live differently each day?

For further study on Jesus as the Lamb of God, read John 1:29,36 and Revelation 7:17; 15:3; 19:9; 22:3.

# PERSONAL STUDY: DAY 3

⭐ **The point: God's judgment is severe and His mercy is great.**

▶ **Read Exodus 12:29-32.**

According to verse 29, whom did God "strike" at midnight?

Underline the phrase "there wasn't a house without someone dead" (v. 30). How did this affect the Egyptians? The Israelites?

What does this tell you about the nature of God's judgment?

What was Pharaoh's reaction? What did he tell Moses and Aaron?

Though this passage reveals God's righteous judgment, it also shows His redeeming power. God's judgment did not discriminate between the rich or poor, the good or bad. In the same way, believers should not choose to share the gospel only with people they know or are comfortable with. God calls us to go to all people (Mark 16:15).

▶ Respond

List the names of two people you know who need to know Jesus. Commit to pray for those people this week, and ask God to give you the opportunity to share the gospel with them.

Maybe you haven't ever shared your testimony, or the story of how you came to know Jesus as Savior, with anyone. In your journal, write a letter to an unsaved friend describing that time in your life. Use the following questions to guide you as you write:

• What made you realize your sinfulness and need for a Savior?
• Were any particular people influential during this time in your life?
• How is your life different now because you know Jesus?

# PERSONAL STUDY: DAY 4

⭐ **The point: God is worthy of praise for His glory.**

▶ **Read Exodus 14:1-14.**

What caused Pharaoh to go after the Israelites? What was God's role in this?

God delivered the Israelites from Egypt and had been present with them through their entire journey. Even though Pharaoh's pursuit of them was also part of God's plan, the people panicked. Reread verses 11-12 and summarize the people's complaints in your own words.

What was Moses' response to their fearful rebellion?

In what way did God assure Moses their helplessness would serve to demonstrate His glory? Explain.

What do you think Moses meant when he said the Israelites only had to be quiet (v. 14)?

▶ **Respond**

Why do you think we are so quick to stress out and worry when life presents problems? What should we do instead? List a few ideas on an index card and keep it with you throughout the week. Whenever you begin to stress, look at the card to remind yourself what you can do instead.

For further study on trusting God in the face of opposition, read 2 Chronicles 20:15-17 and Psalm 106:1-10.

# PERSONAL STUDY: DAY 5

## ✪ The point: God is worthy of praise for His deliverance.

▶ Read Exodus 14:17-18.

In your Bible, highlight each occurrence of the words "I (will) receive glory" (vv. 17,18). What does this indicate about God's reason for allowing the Egyptians to come after His people?

Why is this important?

▶ Read Exodus 14:21-31.

The Egyptians and Israelites both shared the Red Sea experience—in which the Israelites crossed on dry ground and the Egyptians were swallowed up in it when the waters were released. Similarly, during the plagues back in Egypt, both the Israelites and Egyptians witnessed the same miracles, yet their experiences were drastically different.

Describe what the Egyptians experienced as they pursued the Israelites across the Red Sea (vv. 25,28).

What was the experience like for the Israelites?

▶ Respond

When has God delivered you from temptation or danger? Maybe this was the point at which you realized you needed a Savior or a point of decision later on. What was it like to know Him as your Deliverer in that moment?

Did you immediately see God at work in this situation or were you blind to it like the Egyptians? Thank God for revealing Himself to you as your personal Deliverer.

# GOD ESTABLISHES THE WORSHIP OF HIS PEOPLE

*GOD DESIRES TO DWELL AMONG HIS PEOPLE.*

# INTRODUCTION

God's people were delivered from slavery and oppression, not because of their courage, commitment, or righteousness but instead by God's mercy. As judgment fell on Egypt, the people of Israel were saved through a sacrificial substitute. In the same way, we are only saved from the judgment of God through the sacrificial Lamb of God who takes away the sin of the world.

The Israelites had witnessed the power of God to deliver them, but God was just getting started in His renewed relationship with them. God has always desired to live in relationship with His people, both then and now, but His people need to be taught how to relate rightly to Him.

 Why is it comforting to know that God desires to live in relationship with His people?

# SETTING THE CONTEXT

Though God had shown His power and willingness to provide for their needs, the people failed to trust in the manner of His provision. They complained about their lack of food and water, but the Lord, once again, was faithful to provide. God sent manna, a bread-like substance, to rain down from heaven each morning, providing sustenance for the people on a daily basis.

After three months, God brought the people to Mount Sinai, where they would worship Him. God met the people there, but they were terrified at His power displayed through thunder and lightning and a thick cloud on the mountain. God told Moses to set a boundary around the mountain, knowing that because of their sin, the people could not come close to Him and live. But God instructed Moses and gave him the law so the people could know how to worship Him and live according to His commands. These instructions included building "The Tabernacle" (p. 34).

# *THE* **TABERNACLE**

- God showed Moses the pattern for the tabernacle and all of its furnishings (Ex. 25:9).
- God filled Bezalel and Oholiab with wisdom and skill to complete the work and to teach others who also were given wisdom and skill for the construction of the tabernacle (Ex. 35:30–36:1).
- The people of Israel did according to all that the Lord had commanded Moses (Ex. 39:32).

| *EDEN* | | *THE TABERNACLE* |
|---|---|---|
| Genesis 3:8 | **God's Presence** | Exodus 40 |
| Genesis 3:24 | **East-facing Entrance** | Numbers 3:38 |
| Genesis 3:24 | **Guarded by Cherubim** | Exodus 26:31-35 (Cherubim Embroidered in the Veil) |
| Genesis 2:9 | **Tree of Life** | Exodus 25:31-40 (The Golden Lampstand) |

# SESSION VIDEOS

Watch this session's video, and then continue the group discussion using the following guide.

▶ What ideas or phrases stood out to you most in the video? Why?

▶ How should we as Christians view the Ten Commandments?

# GROUP DISCUSSION

**As a group, read Exodus 20:1-8.**

▶ What do these four commandments have in common, and why do you think they come first in the Ten Commandments?

▶ How did Jesus interpret these commands in Matthew 22:34-40?

⭐ What is the connection between obedience and love?

God has no rival, and He has called people to demonstrate their loyalty by giving their highest devotion to Him and no one else. In the garden of Eden, Adam and Eve fell to the temptation to "become like God." In this first commandment, God turns right side up what was turned upside down by human sin. Giving God the place He rightly deserves in our affections is necessary for every action, thought, and relationship.

The second command amplifies the first. In our sin, we who are made in God's image turn around and seek to make Him into ours. We fashion idols and put our trust in them, hoping they will bring us significance and salvation.

▶ What are some of the good things in your life that could easily become idols?

Everything in life begins with loving the Lord. When we love the Lord in the way He commands, obedience to the other commandments, including the commands that deal with our other relationships, flows naturally from that love. Jesus knew obedience begins in the heart, which is why He summarized all of God's law in terms of loving God and loving others.

# GROUP DISCUSSION *CONT.*

As a group, read Exodus 20:12-17.

⭐ How does the way we relate to others connect to our love of God?

▶ Why must we understand the heart issues behind these commandments instead of viewing them as merely outward acts of obedience?

God created the family as the center of human relationships. The Fifth Commandment focuses on these relationships and helps us understand why they are so important. God calls us to honor our parents in response to His redeeming love for us. The Hebrew word translated *honor* means to make weighty and carries a positive sense of giving respect in abundance.

▶ Do you struggle to honor your parents? In what ways?

▶ How would your family life be different if you made the Fifth Commandment more of a priority?

Living in a way that honors God begins in the home, but it extends to other relationships as well. In fact, when Jesus was asked which commandment is the greatest, He summed up the law by calling people to love God with all their heart, soul, and mind, and to love their neighbors as themselves. Paul later spoke of the prohibitions against adultery, murder, stealing, and coveting as summed up by the command to love our neighbors as ourselves (Rom. 13:9-10).

But what does loving our neighbor look like? How do we relate to the people around us? In giving the law, God addressed particular ways that we are to respect and value His likeness reflected in every human being.

▶ How would the world be different if more Christians lived according to the last six commandments?

As a group, read Exodus 40:34-38.

⭐ How did God's presence benefit the people of God?

▶ In what sense does God live among His people today?

▶ What benefits does His presence bring to us?

God showed His desire to be among His people by filling the tabernacle with His glory. When the Holy Spirit came at Pentecost, God took up residence within every believer. The Christian is the new tabernacle in which the Spirit of God dwells, and we can trust Him for guidance, comfort, conviction, and empowerment to live out our gospel mission.

## CHRIST CONNECTION

*The law reveals how we are to live properly in relationship with holy God and others, but because of sin, it is impossible to keep God's law. God sent His Son, Jesus, to "tabernacle," or dwell, with us, and through His life of perfect obedience, His death, and His resurrection, we are forgiven of our sin and credited with His righteousness when we trust in Him.*

# OUR MISSION

 **Head**

How might your own relationship with God influence your relationships with other people?

What might this look like in your own life moving forward?

**Heart**

Why is it right for God to demand first place in our hearts?

What are some ways you might identify personal idols in your own life?

**Hands**

How might our mission as Christ's ambassadors be hindered by dishonoring our parents, stealing, coveting, and so forth?

What might your friends conclude about your walk with Christ if they observe a heart that is content within you?

# PERSONAL STUDY: DAY 1

⭐ **The point: The Israelites believed they were entitled to God's provision.**

Take a minute to review earlier devotions on the exodus. Create a timeline and jot down some of the amazing things God did for the Israelites up to this point on their journey. Begin with the plagues and end with crossing the Red Sea.

▶ **Read Exodus 17:1-2.**

Israel faced impossible odds again and again, and each time they witnessed God's wonders as He provided for them. Still, they complained. In this passage, what was their main complaint?

Based on Moses' response in verse 2, how would you classify their motive in complaining to Moses about the lack of water?

List some common complaints you hear today—at home, church, or with your friends. How could we turn to God and trust Him to provide for us instead?

▶ **Respond**

People often complain when they feel like they deserve something, yet find themselves lacking. This sinful attitude is called entitlement. In today's passage the Israelites felt entitled to God's provision—they were His people and He had provided for them before. It can be easy to fall into the pattern of thinking we deserve what we have or the things we want, but this line of thought doesn't honor God and must be dealt with.

Ask the Holy Spirit to guide you as you examine your heart on this matter. Confess to God any tendency to believe you're entitled to anything He gives to you, whether grace, mercy, love, or something material.

# PERSONAL STUDY: DAY 2

⭐ **The point: The Israelites began to question God's goodness.**

▶ **Read Exodus 17:3-4.**

The Israelites were _____—a real and physical problem. Why do you think they "grumbled against Moses"?

They chose to address this problem by turning against Moses. In doing this, they behaved as if they didn't know their freedom and this journey were part of God's plan. How could they have handled their problem in a way that still honored God?

The Israelites' response indicated a lack of faith in God's goodness. How could Moses' cry to God be seen in the same way?

▶ **Read Psalm 73.**

According to verses 1-12, why did the psalmist doubt God's ways?

How did he overcome this doubt?

What can today's believers learn from the psalmist's words?

▶ **Respond**

This kind of doubt is not uncommon, but we must turn our hearts back toward the bigger picture. Popularity and good fortune in this world mean nothing compared to enjoying the goodness of God. Just as God's plan never included abandoning His promises to Israel, His plan doesn't include abandoning us.

What are some needs you currently have? These may be physical, emotional, or spiritual. Create a list and then take those needs before God in prayer.

# PERSONAL STUDY: DAY 3

⭐ **The point: The Israelites began to question God's presence.**

The Book of Exodus discusses God's presence in various situations (slavery in Egypt, parting the Red Sea, etc.) and forms (Pillar of cloud and fire). List a few other times and ways God's presence was mentioned in Exodus.

▶ **Now, read Exodus 17:5-7.**

List God's instructions to Moses in verse 5.

What was the Israelites' specific complaint in these verses? Why do you think this "tested the LORD"?

▶ **Read 1 Corinthians 10:1-6.**

Which verse referenced the miraculous water the Israelites received? What did Paul call this water?

Summarize the warning for believers in this passage. In what way are these examples for us?

▶ **Respond**

The people had a temporary problem of thirst in the desert, but Moses saw beyond to the bigger problem of their wavering faith in God's presence.

Have you ever doubted God was with you or concerned about your problems? Confess any doubts to God, and ask Him to strengthen your faith in His presence.

Pay attention to things you're tempted to complain about. Jot them down and pray about them each day.

# PERSONAL STUDY: DAY 4

⭐ **The point: Idol-worshipers distort true worship.**

▶ Read Exodus 32:1-6.

While Moses was receiving the Ten Commandments, the Israelites grew more impatient and demanding. They claimed Moses abandoned them and they needed a new god. What did this reveal about their personal trust (or mistrust) in God?

What small acknowledgement did the Israelites give God in verse 4?

The people knew where Moses was, who God was, and what He had done for them. Why do you think they grew impatient with God's purposes?

The people also used the gold God gave to them when they plundered the Egyptians to create this "god." They misused the gifts He had given them. In what way is this another form of idolatry?

In this state of selfishness, the Israelites seemed to acknowledge only what God did for them rather than who He was. How do people respond to God similarly today?

▶ Respond

On a plain piece of paper, jot down a few of the "idols" in your own life. Meditate on the ways God fulfills your life in contrast to idols. Commit to giving up those idols and wholeheartedly following God.

Ask yourself: Am I using my God-given gifts to bring glory to Him or am I using them for my own agenda?

# PERSONAL STUDY: DAY 5

⭐ **The point: We reflect God in how we relate to Him and others**

▶ Read Exodus 32:11-14.

Highlight the word "interceded" in verse 11. An *intercessor* is *someone who takes on the role of mediator, pleading one person's cause to another.* Explain how this helps you better understand Moses' role in this passage.

How did Moses' actions foreshadow the role Christ now fills for us?
(Hint: Read 1 Tim. 2:5.)

God declared the Israelites should be destroyed, and Moses knew their sin deserved God's wrath. So, why did he plead for their forgiveness? Moses claimed two reasons for God to relent in His anger.

First, how did Moses present God's reputation as a valid reason for forgiveness in verse 12?

Second, what promise did Moses claim from God in verse 13?

Moses saw and understood the survival of God's holy people was completely dependent on the character of God, not man. How does this same knowledge affect you?

▶ Respond

When Moses interceded for the people, he appealed to God's character. His intercession was made out of love for God's people and desire for God's glory.

List the names of people you know who may need someone to intercede for them in prayer. Commit to praying for them this week.

Next, jot down some ways you can model your prayers after Moses' prayer for the Israelites.

# GOD'S PEOPLE REBEL

*EVEN THROUGH OUR FAITHLESSNESS, GOD
REMAINS FAITHFUL.*

# INTRODUCTION

Life is hard. Beyond the objective realities that we face in the world like disease, natural disasters, and death, there are other complications that happen along the way. Every day is filled with moments of decision-making. Some are simple, and some will change the course of your life.

Moments of decision come frequently in our lives, and the same was true of the people described in the Bible. As our journey through the story of Scripture continues, we see the children of Israel approach the brink of the promised land. The God who promised to bring salvation to the world through the seed of Abraham has rescued Abraham's descendants from slavery in Egypt. After years of traveling through the wilderness, the Israelites have arrived at the doorstep of the land God promised. But before they enter, they are confronted with a decision that requires faith.

 When have you faced a decision that required faith? What helped or hindered your faith during that time?

# SETTING THE CONTEXT

Despite all of God's provision, presence, and instruction, the complaints of the people that had begun so quickly after crossing the Red Sea began to grow louder, even coming from Aaron and Miriam, two pillars of the Israelite community and Moses' brother and sister. But the people were not merely grumbling against Moses; they were ultimately shaking their fists at God, the One who had appointed Moses and given him authority. None of these grumblings escaped the Lord's notice or discipline.

"Journey to the Promised Land" (p. 46) shows the people finally arrived at the edge of the land of Canaan, the land God had promised to their forefather Abraham. Standing on the southern edge of this land, the people now faced a choice. Would they trust God even in the face of adversity or would they turn back due to their lack of faith?

# JOURNEY TO THE PROMISED LAND

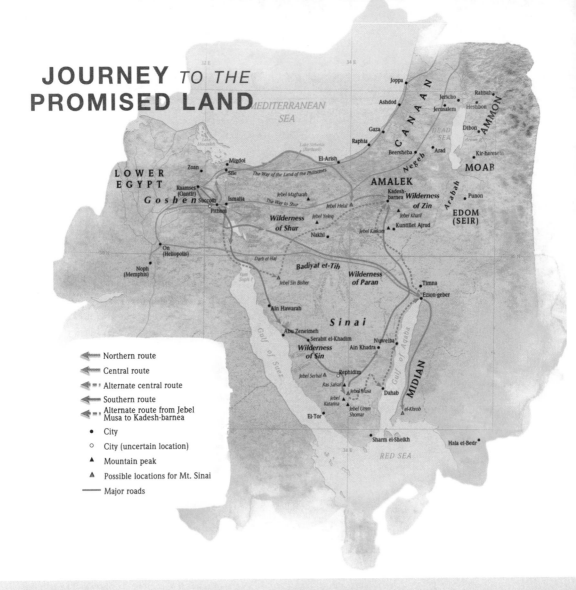

Northern route
Central route
Alternate central route
Southern route
Alternate route from Jebel Musa to Kadesh-barnea
● City
○ City (uncertain location)
▲ Mountain peak
▲ Possible locations for Mt. Sinai
— Major roads

# SESSION VIDEOS

Watch this session's video, and then continue the group discussion using the following guide.

▶ What ideas or phrases stood out to you most in the video? Why?

▶ Why is sin not just a physical act but also an accusation against the character of God?

# GROUP DISCUSSION

As a group, read Numbers 13:1-2, 26-33.

⭐ How is sin related to our faith?

▶ Have you ever been in a situation like this, when it was difficult to exercise faith because of what your senses told you?

▶ What are some promises of God that we need to remember when it is difficult to trust Him?

▶ Make a list of the good things the spies reported about the land, and then make another list of the obstacles mentioned. Which list received more attention? Why?

Consider the incredible report the spies brought back about the beauty of the land. Moses, Aaron, and all of the Hebrews received amazing news. The early part of the spies' report could be summarized like this: "It's better than you can possibly imagine!" They said it was "flowing with milk and honey." The natural resources of the land were like nothing they had seen before.

But, as is often the case we find in the Old Testament, the Israelites faltered in their faith. Right on the heels of describing the land as everything they could hope for, the spies also described why it was impossible to possess. Note the word "however" that shows up in verse 28. With that one word, the spies' report shifted from the goodness of God's promise to the seeming impossibility of possessing the land.

In the face of the dangers present in the promised land, all but two of the spies lost their faith. Joshua and Caleb were ready to forge ahead, but they were outnumbered by spies who believed the fortified cities were too great for God to overcome. When their faith had faltered and their eyes were no longer on the promise, they only saw an unconquerable force before them.

**As a group, read Numbers 14:1-4, 30-35.**

⭐ What lies about the character of God did the people believe?

▶ How might we be tempted to believe similar lies?

▶ In what ways does sin always affect others beyond us?

When the leaders lost their faith, the people of Israel faced a crisis. Once most of the spies said there was no hope, the Israelites went from wondering, to mourning, to outright rebelling. In the heat of the moment, the people's rebellion escalated. They claimed they would be better off dead—a statement which seems ridiculous from where we stand. They wondered whether it would have been better to die in Egypt or in their desert wanderings. Here's a warning for us: The loss of faith includes a loss of good sense. To wish for death when you are on the edge of God's promise is the result of a faithless heart.

▶ What assumptions did the Israelites make? What did their fear reveal about their trust in God? What did it cost them?

▶ How does fear sometimes keep you from following God's plan?

**As a group, read Numbers 21:4-9.**

▶ Why were the complaints of the people so serious? What were they once again charging God with?

▶ How do you see both the justice and mercy of God in this account?

⭐ How do these verses remind us of the gospel?

The people's rebellion in this instance can be summed up in a simple word: impatient. The group of people who had been miraculously delivered, fed, and clothed by God now turned on Him. In essence, they threw a preschooler-like fit before God because they didn't like the food He provided.

The people went far beyond doubt—they accused God and Moses of treachery. They imagined God had intentionally led them out of Egypt for the express purpose of killing them in the desert. It was a rebellion of epic proportions. By stating such a claim, the people showed they doubted God's character and His Word.

▶ When have you become impatient with God? Did your impatience cause you to grumble about what He had or had not done? Explain.

## CHRIST CONNECTION

*God's people rebelled against Him and refused to enter the land He had given them and grumbled about His provision, so He punished them for their continuing disobedience. Because of our sin, we too deserve to be punished by God, but He provided a way of salvation for us through Jesus. When we look with faith upon Jesus Christ lifted high on the cross, we are saved from the punishment of our sin.*

# OUR MISSION

## ○ Head

What does the Israelites' punishment communicate about the
seriousness of sin?

Recall a difficult situation from which God delivered you in the past. How
can reflecting on the ways God has worked in the past give you strength
for your present trials?

## ♥ Heart

In what ways can you see your own heart reflected in the attitude
of the Israelites?

In what types of circumstances do your fears tend to overshadow
your faith?

## ✋ Hands

How effective can we be in sharing our faith if we are like the Israelites
and show a lack of trust and patience with God? What can we do to be
sure that doesn't happen?

What are some ways we can invite others to look to Christ this week?

# PERSONAL STUDY: DAY 1

⭐ **The point: We struggle in our faith when we start looking at our strength instead of God's.**

Consider your own life: When have you tried to accomplish something without God's help? How did that situation work out? How do you think it would have gone differently if you had sought God's will and help in the situation?

▶ Read Numbers 13:1-2,26-33.

Summarize God's command to the Israelites in verse 2.

Underline the phrase "I am giving." What did God's promise indicate about the land He asked them to "scout out" (v. 2)?

List the excuses the men gave for not occupying the land (vv. 28,31-33).

Describe Caleb's response in verse 30. How was his response different from the rest of the men?

▶ Respond

Consider this: When you face challenges in life, are you tempted to focus on your own weaknesses? What do you think would happen if you began to focus on God's strength and ability to get you through the situation instead?

In your journal, list circumstances in your life in which you feel like you're facing impossible odds. Pray over each situation, asking God to help you overcome obstacles to do what He has called you to do.

Israel's military never empowered itself—it's power came from God's hands. In what ways are you tempted to credit yourself with the power to change circumstances? Confess to God any ways you may struggle with this and ask Him to help you acknowledge and fully rely on His strength.

⭐ **The point: We often forget God's past power and promise.**

Before you begin reading today, review yesterday's devotion. The scouts described the promised land as a rich land and as a land filled with giants.

▶ **Read Numbers 14:1-10.**

What was the Israelites' initial reaction to the news from the Scouts (v. 1-2)?

What misconceptions of God's plan did the people hold?

What was the people's proposed solution to the problem of a promised land inhabited by giants?

Describe the reactions of Moses and Aaron, and Joshua and Caleb.

| Moses and Aaron (v. 5) | Joshua and Caleb (v. 6) |
| --- | --- |
| | |

Summarize the way Joshua and Caleb encouraged the Israelites in verses 7-9.

How did God respond to His people?

▶ **Respond**

On a sticky note, jot these down: Don't fear. Don't rebel. Trust God's promise. He will see you through. Place the note somewhere you'll see it every day.

Respond to the following using the headings "Temptations" and "Solutions:"

- In what recent situation were you tempted to fear? How could you turn to God in trust instead?
- In what situations are you tempted to rebel against God? What are some ways you could guard against this?
- In what situations are you tempted to go your own way instead of trusting God?

# PERSONAL STUDY: DAY 3

⭐ **The point: Sometimes believers forget God's promises and become discouraged.**

The Israelites were afraid when they heard the spies' report, despite the fact that God had promised them the land.

▶ **Read Numbers 14:11-12.**

Briefly summarize God's response to His people in verse 11. What does this show you about His character?

According to these verses, in what major way had Israel rebelled against God?

This is a terrifying statement—that God would destroy His people and use Moses' children to build an entirely new covenant people.

Reread the second part of verse 12. What did God's words in verse 12b tell you about His love for His people despite their rebellion?

Even though the people rebelled, God would keep His promise. God promised long before that His people would possess this land (Ex. 3:17). If they would not believe the promise and do as God told them, then God would raise up a people that would. God will always keep His promises.

▶ **Respond**

Reflect on what you truly believe about God in difficult circumstances. Why do you think it's hard to trust Him during those times? How could you change your attitude?

Ask God to give you the courage to trust His promises even when you cannot see the outcome.

For further study on God's promises to believers, read Isaiah 40:29-31; Matthew 11:28-29; and Philippians 4:19.

# PERSONAL STUDY: DAY 4

⭐ **The point: We need a faithful representative to plead for us.**

▶ Read Numbers 14:13-20.

List a few of Moses' reasons for asking God not to wipe out His people.

In verse 18, how did Moses appeal to God's character?

Jot down Moses' final plea to the Lord in your own words.

What was God's response to Moses (v. 20)? Why do you think He responded this way? Why is this important?

▶ Respond

Moses was both an advocate and an intercessor for the Israelites; however, Moses' intercession was only temporary. God's people needed a permanent advocate, so God sent His Son to be our eternal advocate.

Jesus intercedes for us; He is the ultimate faithful representative. However, as His people, we can also intercede for others through prayer. Spend some time praying for people you know who don't know Jesus as Savior or who may be experiencing a difficult situation.

For further study on Jesus as our representative, read Hebrews 1–4.

# PERSONAL STUDY: DAY 5

⭐ **The point: We reflect God in how we relate to Him and others.**

▶ Read Numbers 21:4-9.

God gave the Hebrews freedom from slavery, food they could gather each day, and water—everything they needed. How did the people respond? What were their complaints?

Verse 5 says the people complained against _____ and _____.

What did God send when the people complained? Why?

Reread verse 7. How did the people react to the Lord's discipline?

When God punished the people, they went to Moses. What did they request? What did Moses do?

In verse 8, circle what God told Moses to do and underline what God said the outcome would be. The snake was the punishment for their sin. However, God used another snake to bring healing. Explain verses 8 and 9 in your own words.

▶ Respond

It can be difficult for believers and non-believers alike to hear about the punishment God delivered for sin. However, because of His commitment to redeeming and restoring His people, God must punish and eliminate sin. These events should remind us that sin is costly, but God provided a way for healing and redemption through Jesus Christ.

Consider your own life. Do you have a tendency to complain about the things you have or don't have? Are you ever tempted to blame God for those things?

Take a minute to confess to God any discontent in your own life. Ask Him to help you be content in His love and with His plan for your life in every situation.

# GOD GIVES HIS PEOPLE THE PROMISED LAND

*GOD FIGHTS ON BEHALF OF HIS PEOPLE WHEN THEY RESPOND IN OBEDIENCE.*

# INTRODUCTION

Wimbledon 2001 was the scene of one of the greatest dramatic events ever in tennis—at least for Goran Ivanisevic. The former 1992 Australian Open champion had fallen so far from his glory days that he needed the gift of a wild card to enter the Wimbledon tournament. He and the other players probably thought his presence would not be much more than an uninteresting rerun. He had made it to three previous Wimbledon finals and was the lucky loser each time. This year was different, even though the final included a formidable opponent, double faults, superstition, and doubt. Against all odds, the 125th seeded wild card triumphantly held up the Wimbledon trophy. To say the least, it was an unusual victory.

Joshua 6 contains one of the most dramatic scenes in all of Scripture. There is the protagonist—Israel; the antagonist—the city of Jericho; the rising action—the marching around the walls of Jericho once a day for six days and seven times on the seventh day; and there is the climax—the walls of Jericho come tumbling down! Like Ivanisevic's win many years later, Israel's dramatic victory was against all odds.

 When have you been surprised by the way God worked something out in your life? How does remembering how God has worked in the past help you to trust Him with the future?

# SETTING THE CONTEXT

Throughout those years, the Lord continued to lead His people through Moses. But like the rest of his generation, Moses rebelled against God in the Wilderness of Zin. As a result of his sin, Moses would not be the one to lead them into the promised land.

It was time for a new leader to emerge—Joshua, son of Nun. Joshua had been a military commander for the Israelites. He was also one of the two spies who trusted the Lord to give the Canaanites over to them, despite their great size and strength. Further, Joshua had accompanied Moses as he spoke with God. So at God's command, Moses, before he died, conferred authority onto Joshua as the new leader over Israel.

With a new generation and a new leader, the Israelites stood on the brink of the promised land once again, and the choice of whether or not they would trust God to fight for them was once again before them. "Conquest of the Promised Land" (p. 58) shows that for the most part, they did.

# CONQUEST *OF THE* PROMISED LAND

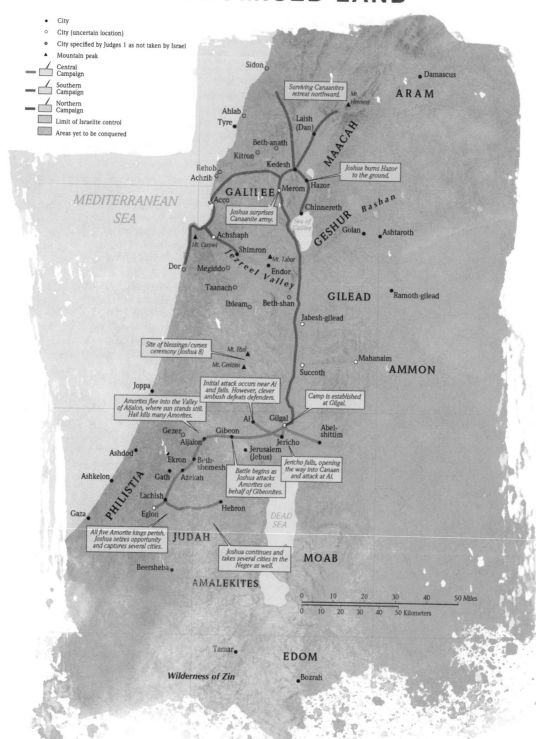

- • City
- ○ City (uncertain location)
- ◉ City specified by Judges 1 as not taken by Israel
- ▲ Mountain peak
- ▬ Central Campaign
- ▬ Southern Campaign
- ▬ Northern Campaign
- Limit of Israelite control
- Areas yet to be conquered

Sidon

Damascus

**ARAM**

*Surviving Canaanites retreat northward.*

Mt. Hermon

Ahlab
Tyre

Laish (Dan)

**MAACAH**

Beth-anath

Kitron

Rehob
Achzib
Kedesh

*Joshua burns Hazor to the ground.*

**GALILEE**
Merom
Hazor

Acco

Chinnereth

**GESHUR** Bashan

*Joshua surprises Canaanite army.*

Sea of Galilee

Golan
Ashtaroth

**MEDITERRANEAN SEA**

Achshaph
Mt. Carmel
Shimron
Mt. Tabor
Endor

Dor
Megiddo
Taanach

*Jezreel Valley*

**GILEAD**
Ramoth-gilead

Ibleam
Beth-shan

Jabesh-gilead

*Site of blessings/curses ceremony (Joshua 8)*
Mt. Ebal
Mt. Gerizim

Mahanaim

**AMMON**

Succoth

Joppa

*Initial attack occurs near Ai and fails. However, clever ambush defeats defenders.*

*Amorites flee into the Valley of Aijalon, where sun stands still. Hail kills many Amorites.*

Ai
Gilgal

*Camp is established at Gilgal.*

Gezer
Aijalon
Gibeon
Jericho
Abel-shittim

Ashdod
Ekron
Beth-shemesh
Jerusalem (Jebus)

*Jericho falls, opening the way into Canaan and attack at Ai.*

Ashkelon
Gath
Azekah

*Battle begins as Joshua attacks Amorites on behalf of Gibeonites.*

**PHILISTIA**
Lachish

Gaza
Eglon
Hebron

**DEAD SEA**

*All five Amorite kings perish. Joshua seizes opportunity and captures several cities.*

**JUDAH**

*Joshua continues and takes several cities in the Negev as well.*

**MOAB**

Beersheba

**AMALEKITES**

| 0 | 10 | 20 | 30 | 40 | 50 Miles |
| 0 | 10 | 20 | 30 | 40 | 50 Kilometers |

Tamar

**EDOM**

*Wilderness of Zin*

Bozrah

58

# SESSION VIDEOS

Watch this session's video, and then continue the group discussion using the following guide.

▶ What ideas or phrases stood out to you most in the video? Why?

▶ Why do you think the people were willing to go forward at this moment while their parents turned back forty years prior?

# GROUP DISCUSSION

As a group, read Joshua 6:1-5.

▶ Put yourself in the place of Joshua. How might you have reacted when you heard God's plan for conquering Jericho?

★ Why do you think God gave the Israelites this battle plan for the first battle they fought in the promised land?

How could marching around the wall of Jericho one time for six days and seven times on the seventh day ever bring down massive walls that were wide enough, according to the ancient historian Josephus, to accommodate driving two chariots side by side? Can you imagine the priests as they listened to Joshua repeat God's instructions? They probably wondered if Joshua was hearing God as well as Moses had heard Him. Surely Joshua had missed a portion of God's instructions, right? Wrong.

God used a seemingly foolish battle plan to accomplish His purpose. As Paul says in the New Testament, "God has chosen what is foolish in the world to shame the wise, and God has chosen what is weak in the world to shame the strong" (1 Cor. 1:27). Throughout this action plan, God will use the Israelites to execute His will and purpose. God's people must participate in the battle of Jericho by marching around the city, and as a result God will give them victory by bringing down the walls. By acting in faith, these massive walls will implode upon themselves without a bulldozer or a wrecking ball because God Himself will bring them down.

# GROUP DISCUSSION *CONT.*

▶ What was God demonstrating to His people, and to the people inhabiting the promised land, through the battle of Jericho?

▶ Have you ever questioned something you sensed God leading you to do? If so, how did you respond?

**As a group, read Joshua 7:1-12, 24-26.**

⭐ What does this account show you about the destructive nature of sin?

▶ How does this story serve as a warning for us?

Joshua usually received his marching orders from the Lord—from how the Israelites were to march across the Jordan River to how they were to march around the walls of Jericho. But this time, he quickly accepted the spies' recommendation to attach Ai and deployed 3,000 men to fight.

In a surprising turn of events, this small city put the Israelites on the run. Apparently, Israel had forgotten that it was not their army who defeated the much larger city of Jericho—it was the Lord who fought for them. They lost the battle at Ai because the Lord was no longer fighting for them.

The reason for Israel's defeat was the presence of rebellion in the camp. A man named Achan had sinned, and God associated Achan's individual sin with the entire community.

Sin is destructive. The sins of individual believers affect the family, the church, and the community. Perhaps others knew what Achan did and allowed it to persist. God told Joshua that He would not fight for him and the Israelites until the correction for their sin had been made.

▶ What are some examples of poor decisions teenagers make that negatively impact their families? their church?

▶ Recall a time when your sin affected more than just yourself. How might considering the impact of your actions help you to obey God and make better choices in the future?

As a group, read Joshua 8:1-2.

⭐ What is encouraging about this word from the Lord, especially in light of Israel's previous defeat?

▶ Why might that encouragement be comforting to the Christian today?

After Joshua had uncovered the sin in the camp, he did not presume success on the battlefield. This time, he listened to the Lord about the number of soldiers who should fight against Ai. God instructed Joshua to take all the soldiers with him and to go to Ai.

The Lord told Joshua that he and Israel would have a second chance as they faced Ai in battle again. The Lord informed Joshua that Ai would suffer what Israel had suffered when there was sin in the camp—defeat.

## CHRIST CONNECTION

*The Valley of Achor is a chilling reminder of sin and its consequences, but God later promises to make the Valley of Achor "a gateway of hope" (Hosea 2:14-15). The wages of sin is death, but the gift of God is eternal life through Jesus Christ our Lord, who has won our victory through His faithful obedience.*

# OUR MISSION

 **Head**

What are some ways we display our faith "in action"?

How does faith "in action" give added credibility to expressing our faith "in words"?

 **Heart**

How should this story help us avoid falling into greed and covetousness?

What are some ways this story has challenged your understanding of personal sin?

 **Hands**

What are some practical ways we can do battle with sin in our lives?

If we become lazy in the fight against sin, how might that become a negative witness to non-believers in our lives?

# PERSONAL STUDY: DAY 1

⭐ **The point: God Himself goes before us.**

▶ Read Joshua 3:5-13.

Summarize the message God gave to Joshua in verses 7 and 8.

Underline the phrase "I will begin to exalt" in verse 7. Would Joshua have to do anything to make himself respected as the new leader of Israel? Why is this important? Explain.

Describe the specific instructions God gave to Joshua to deliver to Israel (vv. 9-13).

| Instructions for the people | Instructions for the priests |
|---|---|
| | |

The ark of the covenant symbolized God's presence among the nation of Israel. Knowing this, how did God physically go before the people? Explain.

How does the Lord go before people today?

▶ Respond

Imagine you were one of the Israelites under Joshua's leadership. What kinds of "wonders" (v. 5) would you anticipate? How does this relate to living in expectation of God's work in your own life?

The Lord is always before us, working on our behalf. Recall a time in your life when you knew without a doubt the Lord was preparing a way for you. Thank Him for His faithfulness to you.

The Lord had already promised Joshua He would go before him. For further study on God's promise to go before His people, read Deuteronomy 31:1-6.

## ✪ The point: God calls us to obey in faith.

Glance back at yesterday's study and recall what the Lord told the priests to do. Summarize God's command to the priests in your own words.

▶ **Read Joshua 3:14-17.**

Reread verse 15. Note the stage of the Jordan during harvest season. Knowing this, what does the Israelites' obedience say about their faith?

What happened when the priests stepped into the water? Sketch the image that comes to mind.

The Israelites obeyed God in faith, and God was faithful to set them safely across the Jordan. What does the phrase "stood firmly on dry ground" (v. 17) say about God's faithfulness?

God doesn't just call us to respond in faith—He makes a way for us and is faithful to see us through whatever He calls us to face.

▶ **Respond**

Consider your own life. What has God called you to do that seemed impossible?

Now, list three situations in which God is currently calling for action. Pray over these, committing to complete and faithful obedience.

For further study on what it looks like to obey in faith, read Genesis 22.

# PERSONAL STUDY: DAY 3

⭐ **The point: God calls us to remember and testify to His power.**

▶ Read Joshua 4:19-24.

What did the Israelites do to remember what they had just experienced? Where did they get the stones? Why is this important?

What was the purpose of the memorial? Do you think they could have remembered and told future generations what happened without this physical reminder? Explain.

Is it still important today for parents and grandparents to spiritually shape the younger generation? Do you see this happening around you? Explain.

Why should the mighty acts of the Lord be remembered and shared with others? Explain.

▶ Respond

List the names of the people who have taught you about God. Pray for them and thank God for their influence in your life.

Do you have a special way of remembering how God works in your life? If not, try keeping a journal or box filled with small items or letters that help you remember. Periodically look through it as a reminder of God's faithfulness.

For further study on remembering God's power, read 1 Samuel 7:1-12.

# PERSONAL STUDY: DAY 4

⭐ **The point: God promised victory over His enemies.**

▶ Read Joshua 6:1-5.

Describe the battle plan in your own words.

Look closely at verse 2. How could Joshua confidently lead the people even though the plan seemed odd? What did this say about Joshua's faith?

What do you think the priests were thinking as they listened to Joshua share the Lord's plan of attack?

How did this strategy focus on God's power rather than the people's ability? Did the Israelites still have a role to play, even though the plan didn't involve military conquest or weapons? Explain.

▶ Respond

Has God ever asked you to do something for Him in a way that seemed strange at the time? How did He reveal His plan to you? His power?

You can be confident that there will always be victory over the enemy where God is concerned. Thank God for the assurance of knowing the battles have already been won.

For further study on God's ways being different than our own, read Isaiah 55:8-11.

# PERSONAL STUDY: DAY 5

⭐ **The point: The people prepare for victory over God's enemies and obey.**

▶ Read Joshua 6:15-21.

The Israelites obeyed God and marched around the wall of Jericho in silence once a day for six days. What changed on the seventh day? Why was that significant?

In your own words, describe Joshua's orders to the people.

Why was it important for the Israelites to destroy everything in the city (v. 17)?

At the sound of all the voices shouting, what happened to the wall?

The Israelites never expressed any inward doubt; they fully obeyed the Lord's instruction and completely trusted Joshua. Why is it important for us to have the same faith in God's plan?

▶ Respond

In what probably seemed like a crazy plan to the people of Jericho, the Israelites trusted God would come through. They trusted His plan. Often, the way God calls believers to live doesn't make sense to the rest of the world. However, just like Israel, we will see His faithfulness in our obedience.

Has God ever asked you to do something that seemed strange, but you obeyed anyway? What did you learn about His character through your obedience?

What sin in your life do you need to destroy in order to obey? Take some time now to confess it to the Lord and ask Him to forgive you so you can live the life of holiness He has called you to.

# THE EARLY JUDGES

*SIN OCCURS WHEN PEOPLE TURN FROM GOD AND DO WHAT THEY THINK IS RIGHT IN THEIR OWN EYES.*

# INTRODUCTION

In 1954, William Golding wrote a novel about a group of well-educated, well-behaved English schoolboys who crash into the paradise of a deserted island with no adult survivors. The book, *Lord of the Flies*, posed the question of whether they would use their privileged upbringing and knowledge to create a new society of peace, or whether the story would go in a different direction.

As the story progresses, we see that instead of creating harmony and peace, these little boys fight for power, hunt and kill each other, and even cut off the head of a pig and sacrifice it to an imaginary and yet utterly real "beast" on the island. Golding uses this beast as a symbol for the evil in the heart of every person, even children, and ultimately shows the consequences of what the world would look like if all rule and authority were removed and rejected.

Golding's book, which sold more than 15 million copies, is popular not because it's so unbelievable but because it's so terrifyingly possible. The underlying moral logic of the story is an imaginary outworking of the truth about the nature and condition of our own hearts. We are a people who constantly reject God's rule and authority over our lives while we make decisions based on our individual beliefs of right and wrong.

# SETTING THE CONTEXT

God's people were on the move. After their incredible victory at Jericho and their surprising defeat at Ai, the Lord continued to move His people further into the promised land. Each foe was defeated before Joshua and the army of Israel, and as they fell, God demonstrated over and over again that He is the only true God. These were more than just battles over land; each victory for Israel was a victory for the Lord over the pagan gods of the Canaanites.

The Israelites were about to settle in a land that had been filled with all kinds of idolatry and was still populated by people who worshiped false gods. The Lord knew that His people would be tempted to integrate the worship of idols into their spiritual lives. The people swore their allegiance, promising they would worship only the God of Israel, but their commitment to God and His covenant was short-lived. It took only one generation before they began to worship foreign gods. Thus began the period of the judges, in which the Israelites fell into a pattern of sin, judgment, repentance, and deliverance, as shown in "The Judges Cycle" (p. 70).

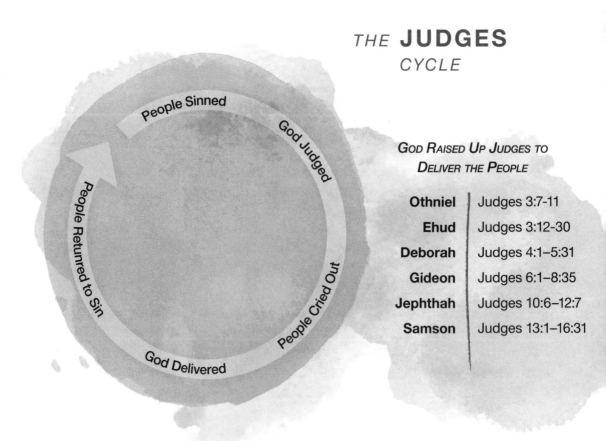

## THE **JUDGES** *CYCLE*

People Sinned

God Judged

People Cried Out

God Delivered

People Returned to Sin

*GOD RAISED UP JUDGES TO DELIVER THE PEOPLE*

| | |
|---|---|
| **Othniel** | Judges 3:7-11 |
| **Ehud** | Judges 3:12-30 |
| **Deborah** | Judges 4:1–5:31 |
| **Gideon** | Judges 6:1–8:35 |
| **Jephthah** | Judges 10:6–12:7 |
| **Samson** | Judges 13:1–16:31 |

# SESSION VIDEOS

Watch this session's video, and then continue the group discussion using the following guide.

▶ What ideas or phrases stood out to you most in the video? Why?

▶ What are some ways we can try to end the cycles of sin in our own lives? In our families? In our churches? In our communities?

# GROUP DISCUSSION

As a group, read Judges 2:8-19.

⭐ How could a generation rise up that did not know the Lord or what He had done?

▶ What does that tell you about our responsibility for the next generation?

▶ What do these verses reveal about our pull toward sin?

Perhaps this serves as a warning to us: Faithfulness to God does not pass from generation to generation through the genes. We don't inherit our parents' salvation, and we can't expect our children to inherit ours. For this reason, we must be diligent to pass on the knowledge of God to the next generation.

It's also important to recognize that we are called not to merely pass on information to the next generation, but to pass on the faith. The problem with this generation of Israelites was not that they did not "know" cognitively what the Lord had done. The problem was that they did not know God personally. "Know" here refers to intimate knowledge. Their relationship with God was not precious to them.

Forgetting the promises of the Lord leads to making decisions apart from Him. They did what was "evil in the Lord's sight." God, not us, determines what is right and good, and what is sin and evil. This is the calling card of sin: We think we know better than God. The Book of Judges may be best known for the last verse of the book that sums up what sin is: "In those days there was no king in Israel; everyone did whatever he wanted" (Judg. 21:25).

▶ Have you ever been unfaithful to God because you were more concerned about yourself than obeying Him? Explain.

**As a group, read Judges 4:4-7.**

▶ What sticks out to you the most about this description of Deborah the judge?

★ What must you believe to be true about God to take a courageous stand for Him?

Before God raised up Deborah as a judge, the people lived under the oppression of King Jabin and his commander Sisera for twenty years. Despite this long period of oppression, Deborah knew that the power of the Lord was stronger than the power of their enemies, and that knowledge gave her the boldness to move forward.

Barak was Deborah's general, and he led the army of God's people. At first glance it might seem like Deborah was filled with faith and Barak with fear, but this was probably not the case. Barak, a mighty general, said he would fight Sisera's army if Deborah, the woman, would go with him. Deborah represented the voice of God in this passage. Barak wanted to know that the word of God would be with him, just as Moses did in Exodus 33 when he begged God to be with the people of Israel.

So Barak demonstrated faith, and he obeyed by preparing an army of 10,000 men. Barak used the gifts God gave him to walk in faithfulness. He knew his role in the story was small and not for his own glory but for the glory of God.

**As a group, read Judges 4:14-16.**

▶ Have you ever felt like Barak, in need of encouragement from someone else to do a difficult thing? What happened?

★ Why might God desire to place us in difficult situations?

▶ What effects can facing difficult situations have on our faith?

The hinge of this story is verse 14: "Hasn't the Lord gone before you?" This was the place of confidence and hope for the people of God: the Lord had gone before them. Deborah and Barak and the people of God had faith in the Lord's words, and He said they would be victorious. Because He is a faithful God, their faith in His victory was secure.

Faith leads us to be courageous when facing impossible odds. Faith is demonstrated by our belief and obedience, our trust in God and desire to obey Him in faith. Our faith is not rooted in our gifts, or found in our skills, or propped up by our ambitions. Our faith is in the word of God and in His unshakable character. As the people of God, we build our lives on the promises of God. No other foundation is stable.

▶ How do you typically respond when you are facing what seem to be impossible odds?

## CHRIST CONNECTION

*The judges saved people from the consequences of their sin but could not change the cause of their sin. Jesus is the Savior and Judge who takes upon Himself the consequences of our sin and then offers us new hearts that seek His righteousness.*

# OUR MISSION

 Head

What are some ways we are tempted to do what is right in our own eyes? What are some examples of our culture living this way?

What are the dangers of deciding for ourselves what is right for me or right for you?

 Heart

What are some modern day idols that we see redirect people's worship away from God?

What are some ways to prevent our hearts from being redirected to these false idols?

 Hands

How do you currently use your giftedness to serve those within your church?

What are some areas where you can begin to start serving and using your gifts for God's kingdom?

# PERSONAL STUDY: DAY 1

⭐ **The point: God punishes evil.**

▶ Read Judges 2:11-15.

According to verses 11-13, what did the Israelites do to make God angry? Why do you think their actions angered Him? Explain.

Reread verse 14. What did God give His people in response to their rebellion?

Summarize verse 15 in your own words.

▶ God is holy and just. He can't allow sin to continue without consequences. Read about God's promise to punish Israel's disobedience in Leviticus 26:14-17.

List the two ways God said He would punish the Israelites if they failed to obey Him.

The Israelites experienced times of intimate relationship with the Lord and periods of rebellion. During both the times of obedience and disobedience, they remained God's chosen people. In what ways does this bring comfort to believers today?

▶ Respond

Read Judges 21:25 and reflect on it as you respond to these questions.

• What are some ways you are tempted to do what is right in your own eyes?
• Have you ever been more concerned about your own desires and plans than obeying God?

Develop a plan to use God's Word to fight against these sinful desires in your own life. Include a few verses to memorize and use in prayer. (Hint: Check out Eph. 6:10-18 and Matt. 4:1-11.)

## ⭐ The point: God saves His people through a chosen leader.

What qualities, characteristics, and words do you usually associate with leaders? Journal your response.

▶ **Read Judges 2:16-19.**

Who "raised up judges" (v. 16)? Why is this important?

In your own words, explain what the judges did (v. 16b).

Use verse 17 to help you fill in the blanks in the following statements.

The Israelites _____ from _____ the Lord's commands.

They did not obey God like their _____ did.

God didn't raise up leaders because of His people's obedience. What reason does verse 18 give for God's provision of judges? What does this say about God's love for His people?

According to verse 19, how did the Israelites act once a judge died? Why do you think they responded in this manner? Do you see people responding in the same way when a leader dies today?

▶ Respond

The downward spiral of sin and disobedience continued despite the judges' calls to repent. We also need a Savior who can free us permanently from the pattern of sin. Through faith in Christ, we have access to this freedom from sin.

Prayerfully consider your own life. Are there times God has delivered you from bad situations, even though you were disobedient to Him in some way? How did that situation affect your relationship with Him?

# PERSONAL STUDY: DAY 3

⭐ **The point: Faith leads us to use our gifts in service to God.**

▶ Read Judges 4:1-7.

Underline the phrase "did what was evil in the sight of the Lord" (v. 1). What do you think this says about the Israelites' belief in God?

According to verse 3, what was the Israelites' response to their oppression?

Underline the phrase "hasn't the Lord … commanded you" (v. 6). Deborah reminded Barak of God's command, and then she reminded Him of God's promise. Summarize the promise of God at the end of verse 7.

▶ Read Romans 12:3-8.

Paul said believers "do not have the same function" (v. 4) in the body of Christ. How can this encourage all believers to use their gifts to serve God? Explain.

List the gifts Paul mentioned in verses 6-8.

▶ Respond

What gifts do you know God has given to you? List a few of your God-given gifts and talents. Then, jot down some ways you could use those gifts to serve God in your church or community.

Deborah used her gift of prophecy and her position as a judge to lead God's people well. Ask God to reveal your gifts to you and to show you how to use them to serve Him.

# PERSONAL STUDY: DAY 4

⭐ **The point: Faith leads to courage and giving God the glory for our victories.**

▶ Read Judges 4:12-16.

Underline the number of chariots Sisera had. He also had many other soldiers with him. Barak had 10,000 men. What would logic tell us about the outcome of this battle? What happened to Sisera's army?

In your own words, jot down Deborah's command to Barak in verse 14.

God fought for the Israelites. How do you think this affected the outcome of the battle? Explain.

▶ Respond

Reflect on challenges you have faced in the past year. Were you sometimes tempted to rely on yourself to make it through? When you conquer a problem in your life, are you tempted to glorify yourself instead of God?

Just as God was the hero in Barak and Deborah's story, Jesus is the hero of our story. Take a minute to jot down a prayer of praise to Jesus for rescuing you from sin.

# PERSONAL STUDY: DAY 5

⭐ **The point: Faith leads to worship as we reflect on God's goodness in our lives.**

▶ Read Judges 5:1-11.

What is the main focus of the praise in these verses?

What's the main characteristic of God that you see in this song?

Sometimes songs are the best way to communicate a story. When Americans attend a sporting event, they stand together and sing a story: "O say, can you see by the dawns early light?" They sing Francis Scott Key's account of the War of 1812. It's war history, and "The Star Spangled Banner" reminds Americans of who they are and their story as a nation. Similar to a national anthem, the song of Deborah and Barak was a victory song.

The focus of this song is not on the characters in the story, but on God as the rescuer. The leaders' egos and the people's accolades fade away in light of the glory of the one true God (4:14). It was the Lord who called Deborah to sit as a judge over His people. It was the Lord who gave Barak skills and leadership to assemble and train an army. It was the Lord who gave Sisera into the hands of a housewife (Jael, the woman who struck down the mighty general with a tent peg). It was the Lord who went out before them.

▶ Respond

We saw in this story the song of Deborah and Barak. It is interesting that other religions aren't known for singing and writing hymns and praise songs. Buddhism, Islam, and Hinduism are not marked by song the way Christianity is. As Christians, we can't seem to help but sing. Our faith sings. And here, after God gave His people the victory, Deborah and Barak broke into song, which is exactly what happens in our own hearts when we reflect on the love of God and His victory over sin in our lives.

What are some Christian songs that cause you to reflect on God's love for us in Jesus, leading you to worship?

How does this story help us think about the circumstances that lead us to worship through song?

# THE LATER JUDGES

*GOD WORKS EVEN THROUGH THE DEFEAT OF
SINFUL LEADERS TO BRING ABOUT HIS PLAN.*

# INTRODUCTION

If you were to put together a winning team, what kinds of people would you select? Perhaps you would look for the biggest, strongest, fastest people, giving you physical advantage over your opponents. Maybe you would choose the smartest and quickest thinkers to give you a mental upper hand. But when you look through Scripture at the team God uses in the unfolding of His plan, it seems like an unlikely collection of people.

All of the characters in Scripture are sinners in need of a Savior: Abraham the doubter, Jacob the deceiver, Moses the murderer, David the adulterer, and Rahab the prostitute. We could go person by person through the entire Bible and see this pattern repeated over and over through redemptive history. God doesn't shy away from working through imperfect people.

 Why do you think the Bible's story line consistently highlights the flaws and failures of its heroes? Why is that significant for us to see?

# SETTING THE CONTEXT

Once in the promised land, the Israelites soon adopted the pagan practices and idols of the people dwelling there. God would bring discipline on His people through oppression from the surrounding peoples, and then they would cry out to Him. In His mercy, God would raise up a deliverer—a judge—to whom He would give amazing insight or abilities for the deliverance of His people.

God's judges started with Othniel, Caleb's youngest brother, who brought peace to the land for forty years. Ehud, the next judge, assassinated King Eglon by stabbing him with such force that the king's fat closed over the hilt of his sword. Deborah, whom we read about in the previous session, gave military counsel which led to victory.

Then came Gideon, an unlikely leader whom God used to defeat the Midianites, as we will see in this session. Jephthah delivered the people but at the cost of his own daughter due to a foolish vow. And of course, Samson was blessed by God with mighty strength to liberate his oppressed people, but he serves as a lasting example of the ultimate failure of all these judges. "Seeing Jesus in the Judges" (p. 82) shows us that Jesus is the greater, perfect Judge who was still to come.

## SEEING
# JESUS IN THE JUDGES

| OLD TESTAMENT | NEW TESTAMENT |
|---|---|
| **The Judges**<br>Saved the People While Still Alive<br>(Judges 2:18) | **Jesus**<br>Saves His People Forever, Being Raised<br>from the Dead (Romans 8) |
| **Gideon's Army of 300**<br>God's Glory Through Weakness<br>(Judges 7:2) | **Preach Christ Crucified**<br>God's Power and Wisdom<br>(1 Corinthians 1:24) |
| **Samson's Death**<br>Vengeance upon His Idolatrous Enemies<br>(Judges 16:28) | **Jesus' Death**<br>Salvation for His Enemies Who Believe<br>(Romans 5:8-10) |
| **Samuel**<br>A Prophet to Whom God Revealed<br>Himself by His Word (1 Samuel 3:21) | **Jesus**<br>In these Last Days God Has Spoken to<br>Us by His Son (Hebrews 1:2) |

# SESSION VIDEOS

Watch this session's video, and then continue the group discussion using the following guide.

▶ What ideas or phrases stood out to you most in the video? Why?

▶ How do the judges show us that we need the perfect Judge in Jesus?

# GROUP DISCUSSION

**As a group, read Judges 6:11-16.**

▶ What is strange about the way the angel addressed Gideon?

⭐ What other biblical accounts does this conversation between the angel and Gideon remind you of?

▶ Do you think there is a difference between how God sees you and how you see yourself? If so, what is it?

When God came to Gideon, he made an incredible promise to him: "The Lord is with you." Notice how this section begins with the angel of the Lord assuring Gideon of God's presence and ends with the same promise. Surprisingly, Gideon responded by questioning God's promise. If God was with them, then why had He allowed Midian to oppress them?

Like Gideon, we sometimes fail to see our sin and guilt, so we rush to blame God for whatever trials or suffering we are going through. Sometimes, our difficult circumstances are brought about by our own sinfulness, not because God has been unfaithful. Gideon's perspective shows why God first sent the word of a prophet—He wanted His people to know they were at fault and needed deliverance.

Next, Gideon protested against God's commission on the basis of his inadequacy ("I am the youngest in my father's house!"). God's response ("I will be with you") was a reminder that the power of deliverance was not in Gideon, but in God's presence. The scene reminds us of how Moses responded when God commissioned him. In both cases, the problem is one of perspective. Both Gideon and Moses first looked to themselves for their source of strength and acknowledged their deficiency. But God called them to turn their eyes to Him and His perfect ability.

▶ What is something you've faced in the past that you didn't understand? How did it affect your faith?

Prior to these verses, God had whittled down Gideon's army to a fraction of its previous size. Based on size alone, the army of Israel would be no match for Midian. But God was positioning Gideon and the army to demonstrate that the battle truly belonged to Him.

**As a group, read Judges 7:15-22.**

⭐ What does this victory demonstrate about the way God chooses to do His work?

The victory of Israel over Midian is one of the most extraordinary battle accounts in the Old Testament. In Judges 7:1-8, God pared the army down from 32,000 to 300 men. God insisted that His people see their cause as utterly hopeless, so that they would recognize that their deliverance could only be chalked up to God's power and mercy. Along the way, God continued to reassure Gideon. And finally, Gideon worshipped God as a sign of his faith and trust in God to accomplish His will through him.

God accomplished a unique and grand victory solely through His strength and wisdom. Even the manner of victory showed that the battle belonged to the Lord and that He had accomplished the victory. The 300 men did not even attack; they pursued after the Midianites fled.

▶ What might God be calling you to do that doesn't make sense from an earthly standpoint?

**As a group, read Judges 16:21-22, 26-30.**

▶ How do these passages compare with the vision of Samson as a super-strong warrior for God?

⭐ How does Samson's death between two pillars compare with Jesus' on the cross between two thieves?

▶ Why do you think God chose to empower Samson at this moment, in spite of his faithlessness and disobedience?

Samson's story is a classic tragedy. As his life came to an end, Samson experienced true faith and repentance. He stopped trusting in his own strength and put his hope in God. Here, we find strength in Samson's weakness; it is through man's brokenness that God puts His own glory on display. At the end of his life, Samson cried out to God for enough strength to defeat the enemies of God's people. God reached down into the brokenness of the judge who was chosen before his birth, and for the good of His people, He answered Samson's prayer. He rescued His people despite their total unbelief. Samson's downfall was the result of his own disobedience, yet God used his death to begin the deliverance of His people.

▶ It took humiliation and weakness to finally get Samson's attention. What are some circumstances God can use (or has used) to get our attention and draw us back to Him?

## CHRIST CONNECTION

*The judges were imperfect people whom God used in unexpected ways to deliver His people and show that He is the source of salvation. Jesus was the perfect Rescuer who defeated sin and death in an unexpected way to show everyone that salvation belongs to God alone. God used Christ's death and resurrection to bring deliverance "once for all" for His people.*

# OUR MISSION

**Q** Head

What hope does it give us to see Samson mentioned as a man of faith in Hebrews 11?

What does Samson's story teach us about the patient love and mercy of God?

**V** Heart

Why shouldn't we live a "minimalist Christianity," which is essentially the mind-set that asks of us only the bare amount one can do and still be a Christian?

Like Samson's actions reflecting his heart not being in the right place, what have your actions communicated about your heart recently?

**✋** Hands

How does God's presence influence the way we fight sin in our lives?

How does the story of Samson encourage you to use your God-given gifts for His glory and not your own?

# PERSONAL STUDY: DAY 1

## ⭐ The point: Our strength comes from God.

▶ Read Judges 6:11-16.

Summarize verse 12 in your own words. What is significant about the angel's initial greeting?

Gideon protested because he felt as though the Lord had abandoned His people. How did the Lord respond in verse 14?

What two excuses did Gideon make? How do you think God could demonstrate His strength through Gideon's weaknesses?

This interaction began and ended with the same promise of God's presence. God called Gideon to move his focus from his own inabilities to God's sovereignty. Only when he trusted God could Gideon complete the task ahead of him.

▶ Respond

What aspects of obedience to God's mission make you feel inadequate, or not up to the task?

When do you most often need to be reminded that God is with you? Thank God for His presence. Ask Him to help you see Him at work in your life this week.

On an index card, jot down a Bible verse that emphasizes God's presence. Place the card where you will see it often.

## ✪ The point: Our assurance comes from God.

▶ Read Judges 6:36-40.

Describe the first sign and the second sign Gideon asked for from God.

First Sign

Second Sign

Why do you think Gideon requested a second sign? What does this reveal about his faith?

What does God's willingness to perform two signs teach us about His character?

Instead of asking for a sign, how should believers respond to fears and doubts today?

▶ Respond

The same God who called Gideon to deliver the Israelites calls us into action today. Ask the Holy Spirit to guide you as you examine your heart. Do you sense God calling you to something specific? Confess anything that might hold you back and ask God to give you the strength to follow Him without question.

When God has called you to do something, have you ever been tempted to give excuses? In what ways did God show patience with you?

# PERSONAL STUDY: DAY 3

⭐ **The point: Our victory comes from God.**

List some of the truths you've learned as you studied the Book of Judges this week.

▶ **Read Judges 7:16-22.**

Gideon only had _____ men. He gave them a _____ and an empty pitcher with a _____ inside. What does this tell you about the military strength of Israel during this battle? Why is that important?

Highlight verse 17. What does this tell you about the type of leader Gideon was?

In verse 18, Gideon indicated that the battle was for God. How do you think this designation affected the outcome of the battle?

What do you think Gideon's men learned about God from this battle?

The greatest example of God's victory through our weakness was through Jesus on the cross. How does this passage help believers better understand God's power in our lives today?

▶ Respond

Often we "put on a brave face" or we "fake it 'til we make it." How does faking our strength diminish the appearance of the strength of God? What do you think admitting our weaknesses does to our testimony?

⭐ **The point: Samson's impulses led him to break his vows.**

▶ **Read Judges 14:1-9.**

According to verse 3, why do you think Samson's parents wanted him to find a wife from his own people? Explain.

Reread verse 4. Underline God's plan for Samson involving the Philistine woman.

▶ **Read Judges 16:4-20.**

According to verse 5, for what reason did the Philistines want Delilah to persuade Samson to tell her how he received his strength?

Briefly summarize the lies Samson told Delilah when she asked about the source of his strength.

| v. 7 | v. 11 | v. 13b |
|------|-------|--------|

What was the outcome in each of those situations? What was Delilah's response to Samson?

According to verses 19 and 20, what Nazirite vow did Samson break this time? Describe the major consequence listed in verse 20.

In both instances when Samson broke his vows, where was his focus?

▶ **Respond**

In what ways are you, like Samson, tempted to place your desires above your commitment to God?

# PERSONAL STUDY: DAY 5

⭐ **The point: Samson's defeat leads him to turn back to God.**

Review yesterday's devotion before you begin reading today's Scripture. When Samson broke his vow to God, God left him (Judg. 16:20).

▶ **Read Judges 16:21-30.**

According to verses 21 and 25, what did Samson have to endure at the hands of the Philistines?

Whom did the Philistines praise for their victory over Samson? Why do you think this is important in relation to the Lord strengthening Samson once more?

Summarize Samson's cry to God in verse 28.

What did Samson do after he turned back to the Lord (vv. 29-30)?

Despite his brokenness and failures, God still used Samson to begin delivering Israel from the Philistines. Samson is listed among the heroes of faith in Hebrews 11 because, in his dying act, he acknowledged his strength came from the Lord.

▶ **Respond**

God loves us unconditionally and is able to use us in mighty ways despite our mistakes.

Do you sometimes struggle to believe God could use you to do His work? Why or why not?

If so, confess your struggle to God. Ask Him to help you believe He can use you for His glory.

# HOW TO USE THE LEADER GUIDE

## Prepare to Lead

The Leader Guide is designed to be cut out along the dotted line so you, the leader, can have this front-and-back page with you as you lead your group through the session.

*Watch the session video* and *read through the session content* with the Leader Guide cut-out in hand and notice how it supplements each section of the study.

Use the *Session Objective* in the Leader Guide to help focus your preparation and leadership in the group session.

## Questions & Answers

⭐ Questions in the session content with this icon have some sample answers provided in the Leader Guide, if needed, to help you jump-start or steer the conversation.

## Setting the Context

This section of the session always has an *infographic* on the opposite page. The Leader Guide provides an activity to help your group members interact with the content communicated through the infographic.

## Group Discussion

The Group Discussion contains the main teaching content for each session, providing questions for students to interact with as you move through the biblical passages. Some of these questions will have suggested answers in the Leader Guide.

## Our Mission ◉ ◉ ◉

The Our Mission is a summary application section designed to highlight how the biblical passages being studied challenge the way we think, feel, and live today. Some of these questions will have suggested answers in the Leader Guide.

## Pray

Conclude each group session with a prayer. A brief sample prayer is provided at the end of each Leader Guide cut-out.

# SESSION 1 • LEADER GUIDE

## Session Objective

Show that God was at work to deliver His people from slavery in Egypt and return them to the land of promise He had given them through Abraham. (This session will take them to the brink of deliverance, so it will feel like part 1 of 2 in some ways.)

## Introducing the Study

Use the intro option to highlight the power Egypt had as a political entity at this time.

## Setting the Context

Use the following activity to help group members see how Moses' example means we are also able to be used by God in His mission.

Encourage group members to read over "Moses' Life" (p. 10).

• Ask: "Looking at the first eighty years of Moses' life, what difficulties would you expect him to have as a leader in God's plan?" (Moses was spared from the oppression of his people for forty years as Pharaoh's grandson. Moses murdered an Egyptian taskmaster and then fled away from his people in fear. Moses lived in Midian away from the oppression of his people for another forty years. Moses had a foreign wife.)

• Ask: "If God could overcome all of these obstacles in Moses' life, why do we continue to believe God can't or shouldn't use us?" (Because we struggle to believe in the grace and power of God. We often succumb to the shame and fear of our own sins. We believe there are limits to God's faithfulness.)

*Read this paragraph to transition to the next part of the study:*

Regardless of our excuses, God is the great "I AM"; He is everything we need to live as holy and obedient children. We know this because of how He used Moses, but even more so because He has given us Jesus to rescue us from our slavery to sin.

## Group Discussion

Watch this session's video, and then as part of the group discussion, use these answers as needed for the questions highlighted in this section.

⭐ What is evident about the character of God from these verses? *1) God is gracious and sovereign to use whom He wills. 2) Though God appears to delay, He is faithful to fulfill His promises. 3) God always hears the cries of His people.*

⭐ How might God's answers to Moses encourage you when you feel unqualified? *1) God's presence with me matters more than my ability, or the lack thereof. 2) The goal of obedience to God is worship to His great name, not to mine. 3) God is everything we need for strength and obedience to do what He has called us to do.*

⭐ What would these signs have demonstrated both to God's people and the Egyptians? *1) God is in control over His creation. 2) God's people would have seen that their oppressors were not as strong as they perceived them to be. 3) The Egyptians would have been confronted with the weakness of their so-called gods and religious system.*

## Our Mission

🔵 What are some ways we can increase our sense of reverence for God? *When Moses encountered God, the Scripture says Moses "hid his face." Why? Because Moses was in the presence of the Holy One. We should understand Moses' fear. We should also maintain a sense of reverence before God. However, as believers we don't have to hide from God in fear because of the work of Christ. We are hidden in Him! We can seek God with confidence because of Christ.*

🔵 How is it that sin causes us to turn our hearts from God and His Word? *In Exodus 7, the text says on a few occasions that Pharaoh's heart was hardened (vv. 14,22), which consequently prevented him from listening to the word of the Lord. Instead of allowing the series of plagues to convince him to release the Israelites, Pharaoh continued to resist the word of the Lord, and therefore became more hardened as a result. Eventually, God gave him over to the hardening of his own heart, which resulted in his own death.*

## Pray

Close your group in prayer, thanking God for His ongoing presence in our lives and confessing His greatness over every false god.

# SESSION 2 • LEADER GUIDE

## Session Objective

Show God's final acts of deliverance from Egypt and how the Passover lamb is a type of Jesus, who would be given as the Lamb who takes away the sin of the world.

## Introducing the Study

Use this option as an introduction to talk about the passover.

## Setting the Context

Use the following activity to help group members see the significance of a Christ-centered reading of Scripture.

Instruct group members to review the connections on "Seeing Jesus in the Exodus" (p. 22). Then ask the following questions: "Which connection stands out to you the most? Why?" "What do you make of the wide array of connections between the Old Testament and the New Testament: Jesus with God, a human being, a nation of people, and a sacrificial animal?"

Remind your group that the Bible is telling God's story of His creation and work in the world, and that story centers upon Jesus Christ. From the beginning and here, through the exodus, God was working to prepare people's hearts and minds to see and recognize Jesus for who He is—the promised Son of God sent to save His people from their sin, and all who come to Christ in faith are included as part of His people.

## Group Discussion

Watch this session's video, and then as part of the group discussion, use these answers as needed for the questions highlighted in this section.

⭐ What are some things we might be trusting in to keep us safe? *1) Our good works compared to our bad works. 2) The faith of our parents. 3) Our baptism and church attendance.*

⭐ How do these verses reveal the severity of sin? *1) Sin is a matter of life and death. 2) These verses echo God's warning in the garden that the wages of sin is death. 3) No one can escape the judgment of God against sin without falling upon His grace and mercy.*

⭐ In what ways are we like the Israelites in this manner? *1) We have experienced the grace of God in our salvation from sin, yet we can be timid and fearful to share the gospel with others. 2) We have felt the power of God when we turn away from temptation, yet we still find ourselves struggling with temptation and sin. 3) We've seen unlikely transformation in ourselves and our brothers and sisters in Christ, but we can still despair that a loved one seems beyond God's reach.*

## Our Mission

◯ Why is it sometimes difficult to trust God's guidance? What are some things we learn as we walk by faith in God's guidance? *Like the Israelites who doubted God, we too are tempted not to trust His wisdom and goodness toward us as we face many of life's difficult circumstances. While it's often hard to make sense of things in our own minds because we are not God and cannot see the big picture like He does, we can have full assurance that God knows what He is doing, and we can trust Him to get us where we need to be.*

♥ What is the connection between our worship of the Lamb, Jesus, and our witness to the gospel? *In Exodus 12:27b-28, notice the people's reaction to the Passover instructions: worship and obedience. They "bowed down and worshiped. They did just as the Lord had commanded Moses and Aaron." This theme of worship and obedience runs right through Exodus. By remembering who God is and what He has done, they give God praise and obedience.*

## Pray

Close your group in prayer, praising God for how He has delivered us in Christ and will keep us eternally safe in Him.

# SESSION 3 · LEADER GUIDE

## Session Objective

Show how God was developing a relationship with His people as they traveled from Egypt toward the promised land, starting with instructions for how they could properly worship Him through obedience and sacrifices.

## Introducing the Study

Use this section as an opportunity to talk about how it has always been God's desire to dwell among His people.

## Setting the Context

Use the following activity to help group members see how Eden, the tabernacle, and Jesus all connect with one another.

Allow group members a moment to review "The Tabernacle" (p. 34). Then ask the following questions: "If you were to build a structure for God's presence, would you build an elaborate tent? Why or why not?" "Why do you think the tabernacle mirrors the garden of Eden?" "How does the Scripture that says Jesus 'dwelt,' or 'tabernacled,' among us (John 1:14) affect your perception of this tent?"

Explain that God's presence with His people and the revelation of His glory have been the heart of God since the beginning of His creation. Sin separates God's image-bearers from the One they are to reflect, but in the tabernacle, and supremely in Jesus, God has taken steps to overcome His people's sin and to dwell with them once more.

## Group Discussion

Watch this session's video, and then as part of the group discussion, use these answers as needed for the questions highlighted in this section.

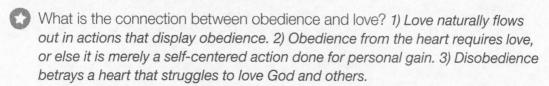 What is the connection between obedience and love? *1) Love naturally flows out in actions that display obedience. 2) Obedience from the heart requires love, or else it is merely a self-centered action done for personal gain. 3) Disobedience betrays a heart that struggles to love God and others.*

⭐ How does the way we relate to others connect to our love of God? *1) We demonstrate our love for God by obeying His commands, so relating rightly to others demonstrates our love for God. 2) We love because He first loved us, so the source of our love for others comes from God Himself. 3) Love for God will drive us to treat others kindly and to seek to make things right when we have wronged others.*

⭐ How did God's presence benefit the people of God? *1) The people knew God was with them every step of their journey to the promised land. 2) God visibly provided the people with direction and rest through His presence in the tabernacle. 3) God provided light to the Israelites during nighttime through a fire in the cloud of His glory.*

## Our Mission

⭕ How might your own relationship with God influence your relationships with other people? *The first four commandments deal with our relationship with God, and the remaining six commandments deal with our relationship with other people. This ordering of God first and then others is important. When you think about it, our relationship with God will determine the quality and extent of our relationships with other people. If that first relationship is healthy and centered on Jesus, then the grace, mercy, and love that He gives will carry over into relationships with other people.*

🔻 Why is it right for God to demand first place in our hearts? *You and I may not struggle with making statues or images of gods to give our attention and devotion, but we should be on guard for idolatry in its more subtle forms. An idol can be anything or anyone that we give first place in our lives. In fact, the most common idols are good things that we make the ultimate thing. The first two commandments remind us that God is a loving and jealous God who will tolerate no rivals to His throne. He must be first in our lives.*

## Pray

Close your group in prayer, thanking God not only for showing us how to live but, through Jesus and the Holy Spirit, giving us the power to do so.

# SESSION 4 · LEADER GUIDE

## Session Objective

Show that even though God had delivered His people and showed them how to have a relationship with Him, they turned from Him and rebelled repeatedly, echoing the ripples of sin we saw from the fall of humanity in the garden of Eden. Once again we see how hopeless our condition is because of our sin.

## Introducing the Study

Use this option to describe the situation the Israelites faced upon entering the promised land.

## Setting the Context

Use the following activity to help group members see God's purposes in the journey.

Ask group members to find the two roads from Egypt to Canaan on "Journey to the Promised Land" (p. 46). Say: "The quickest route between two points is a straight line, or in this case, a paved one, but quickest is not always best or right. God had purposes beyond ease in leading the people in the ways that He did." Then ask the following questions: "What did the people learn from the 'dead end' path to the Red Sea?" "What might the people have learned by going out of the way to Mount Sinai?" "How should God's faithful, daily provision of food for the people have prepared them when they reached the edge of the promised land?"

God teaches His people through more than just instruction and law; He teaches them on the journey. The paths on which God leads us prepare us for future journeys, and the lessons we learn reveal who God is and who we are. We must learn from these lessons and learn from the mistakes of those who went before us. (See 1 Cor. 10:1-13.)

## Group Discussion

Watch this session's video, and then as part of the group discussion, use these answers as needed for the questions highlighted in this section.

⭐ How is sin related to our faith? *1) Sin is the absence of faith or failing to act in faith. 2) "Without faith it is impossible to please God" (Heb. 11:6), which is the essence of sin. 3) Good works without faith are sinful at their core because they are not done for the glory of God.*

⭐ What lies about the character of God did the people believe? *1) The people believed God was deceitful and malicious. 2) The people believed God was weak and helpless against the peoples of Canaan. 3) The people believed God was unfaithful to His promises to Abraham, Isaac, and Jacob.*

⭐ How do these verses remind us of the gospel? *1) "The wages of sin is death" (Rom. 6:23). 2) Ultimate salvation requires that the serpent be crushed (Gen. 3:15). 3) Everyone who looks in faith to Jesus, who was lifted up on a cross, will not perish but have eternal life (John 3:16).*

## Our Mission

🅠 What does the Israelites' punishment communicate about the seriousness of sin? *At the very least, this story communicates once again the weightiness of sin and how all sin is deserving of death. Not only that, but any punishment less than the deserved punishment of death is mercy and grace.*

🅥 In what ways can you see your own heart reflected in the attitude of the Israelites? *The Israelite spies lost sight of their identity as the people of God. They were the people of promise, saved by God and commissioned to take the land He had for them. Instead, they saw some really large soldiers and made a poor assessment of themselves. "Like grasshoppers" is how they saw themselves, but that is not how the Lord saw them. A failure of faith is not only losing faith in God's power, but losing a sense of yourself as His child.*

## Pray

Close your group in prayer, asking God to help you and your group combat sin with faith in His good character and provision.

# SESSION 5 • LEADER GUIDE

## Session Objective

Show how God brought about victory for His people in the land using the battles of Jericho and Ai as examples of the greater conquest and how Israel needed to trust God to fight for them.

## Introducing the Study

Use this option to illustrate the surprising work of God in the lives of the Israelites during this time.

## Setting the Context

Use the following activity to help group members see that God was with His people as they entered and conquered the promised land, just as He had said.

Ask group members to call out some significant details from the map "Conquest of the Promised Land" (p. 58), which might include clear ways the Lord was fighting for the Israelites, the overwhelming success of the Israelites in their battles even though they had been wandering in the wilderness for forty years, the singular defeat at Ai, and the breadth of area yet to be conquered in the promised land. Then ask the following question: "How does the success of these campaigns in the promised land relate to the fears of the previous generation of Israelites forty years earlier?

*Read this paragraph to transition to the next part of the study:*

Forty years earlier, the Israelites rejected the promised land for fear of its inhabitants rather than trusting in the God who had liberated and cared for them. Then after recognizing their folly, they rejected the Lord's discipline and entered the promised land to conquer it but failed because the Lord was not with them. The Bible passages in this session deal with Joshua's central campaign, the victory over Jericho and the defeat then victory over Ai, and the fate of their battles depended upon the Lord's presence.

## Group Discussion

Watch this session's video, and then as part of the group discussion, use these answers as needed for the questions highlighted in this section.

⭐ Why do you think God gave the Israelites this battle plan for the first battle they fought in the promised land? *1) God wanted to prove to the Israelites* that He was going to fight for them. 2) God wanted all the glory from the battle to go to Himself. 3) God wanted the Israelites to retain a humble and obedient posture in their new land.

⭐ What does this account show you about the destructive nature of sin? *1) Sin has a wider range of consequences than we can imagine. 2) Tolerating and condoning sin is disastrous, both for the sinner and the enabler. 3) Secret sins are known to the Lord, and He will judge them.*

⭐ What is encouraging about this word from the Lord, especially in light of Israel's previous defeat? *1) Having dealt with the sin in the camp, the Lord spoke to the Israelites as before, with comfort and encouragement. 2) The people had lost a battle, but they had not lost the war, and the Lord was still fighting for them. 3) The Lord had the battle in hand, and He would grant victory to the people if they would obey.*

## Our Mission

⭕ What are some ways we display our faith "in action"? *God's instructions to the Israelites reveal the importance of words and actions. The people could not utter a word until Joshua gave the order to shout at the sound of the long trumpet blast. Perhaps God wanted the Israelites to display their faith in action before speaking with others about the importance of "faith in action."*

▼ What are some ways this story has challenged your understanding of personal sin? *Achan hid these treasures in his tent. It is possible that his family saw him do this. Perhaps they thought it more honorable to keep Achan's secret than risk alienation by divulging his sin. By hiding his wrongdoing, Achan looked innocent on the outside. However, the inside of his tent revealed otherwise. First Samuel 16:7 declares, "man sees what is visible, but the Lord sees the heart" and Psalm 51:6 states that God desires "integrity in the inner self."*

## Pray

Close your group in prayer, thanking God for His willingness to give the greatest victory of salvation to His children, dependent not on our goodness but on His grace.

# SESSION 6 · LEADER GUIDE

## Session Objective

Show how God's people continued in a tailspin of sin and rebellion against Him, yet in His mercy and kindness, He provided judges to rescue them. While these judges pointed the people back to God, they could not address their own sin problem, which is why the cycle of sin continued.

## Introducing the Study

Use this option to illustrate that living rightly isn't due to being educated or financially well-off, but rather comes from a changed heart that is fully devoted to God.

## Setting the Context

Use the following activity to help group members see the futility of freedom without addressing the heart of sin.

Instruct group members to look at "The Judges Cycle" (p. 70), and then call for six volunteers to read some brief passages from the Book of Judges. These passages detail the first three phases of the Judges cycle with the six main judges named at the bottom of the infographic. (Encourage the volunteers not to stress about the names, just to give them a good try and move on.): Judges 3:7-9a // Judges 3:12-15a // Judges 4:1-3 // Judges 6:1-6 // Judges 10:6-10 // Judges 13:1

Ask: "What are your impressions of the Israelites after reading those passages back to back?" "What are some ways we might fall into a similar cycle?"

Conclude this activity by reading the "CHRIST Connection" (p. 73).

## Group Discussion

Watch this session's video, and then as part of the group discussion, use these answers as needed for the questions highlighted in this section.

⭐ How could a generation rise up that did not know the Lord or what He had done? *1) The Israelites did not pass on their stories of faith and God's faithfulness to their children. 2) The Israelites failed to obey God's command to teach their children the ways of God. 3) The next generation may have rejected what was taught to them by their parents, seeing a more enticing form of religion from their pagan neighbors.*

⭐ What must you believe to be true about God to take a courageous stand for Him? *1) That God is all-powerful and He protects His people. 2) That God keeps His promises and that no matter the consequences from a courageous stand for Him in this life, eternal life will make all those consequences pale in comparison. 3) That God exists and rewards those who seek Him (Heb. 11:6).*

⭐ Why might God actually desire to place us in difficult situations? *1) Difficult situations challenge our faith and help to strengthen our faith in God. 2) Difficult situations provide a unique opportunity for God to demonstrate His power and glory to and through His people. 3) Those who would enjoy seeing or placing Christians in difficult situations can be shocked and convicted when the Lord comes through for His people.*

## Our Mission

⭕ What are the dangers of deciding for ourselves what is right for me or right for you? *The time of Judges is really no different than our own when it comes to moral relativism—the belief that objective right or wrong doesn't exist, but rather people get to decide for themselves what is true, right, and wrong. Of course, this notion of relativism is absurd both logically (it is self-contradictory) and morally (it is really difficult to live out the belief that nothing is objectively wrong in the face of racism, human trafficking, the Holocaust, etc.). Relativism fails not only on account of these arguments and many more but primarily on account that God exists, and He alone determines what is true, right, and wrong.*

⭕ What are some modern day idols that we see redirect people's worship away from God? *One of the interesting things about sin is the fact that it doesn't stop people from worshiping. In the case of the Israelites, we don't see them stop worshiping altogether—they only stop worshiping God. The people worshiped idols instead. Thus, sin is not the ceasing of worship but the sinful redirection of worship away from God and toward idols. Sin, at its root, is a worship problem, which makes it a heart problem.*

## Pray

Close your group in prayer, praying that God will give you courage to live in holiness no matter what excuses you might want to make.

# SESSION 7 · LEADER GUIDE

## Session Objective

Show that God provided what the judges lacked so that it would be clear that salvation is truly from God, and show the inverse function of how the later judges looked like greater rescuers but in reality proved to be less able to deliver God's people, demonstrating the need for the perfect Judge who was to come.

## Introducing the Study

Use this intro to discuss the biblical theme of God using imperfect people to carry out His plan of redemption.

## Setting the Context

Use the following activity to help group members see that both the strength and the weakness of the judges points to Jesus as the greater Judge.

Encourage group members to review the Old Testament and New Testament connections on "Seeing Jesus in the Judges" (p. 82). Ask: "What do the statements about Gideon and Samson call to mind regarding stories told in popular culture?" "Why does human weakness reveal God's strength and glory?" "Why does human strength ultimately reveal human weakness?"

Emphasize the first point that the work of the judges lasted only as long as they were alive, like so much work done by people today. But Jesus' work on the cross lives on with Him and for us because He was raised from the dead, having defeated sin and death.

## Group Discussion

Watch this session's video, and then as part of the group discussion, use these answers as needed for the questions highlighted in this section.

⭐ What other biblical accounts does this conversation between the angel and Gideon remind you of? *1) Abraham questioned how God could provide him with a son when he and Sarah were so old. 2) Moses wanted God to choose someone else as His spokesperson because he felt ill-equipped and afraid. 3) Joshua questioned the plan of God when the Israelites were defeated at Ai, believing the Canaanites would rally together and destroy them.*

⭐ What does this victory demonstrate about the way God chooses to do His work? *1) God works in such a way as to humble His people and bring Himself glory. 2) God works through the obedience of His people, even when that obedience doesn't make sense given the circumstances. 3) No enemy and no army can prevail over God's people when He fights for them.*

⭐ How does Samson's death between two pillars compare with Jesus' on the cross between two thieves? *1) In his strength, Samson died getting vengeance against his enemies; Jesus died calling for forgiveness for those who were crucifying Him. 2) Samson's death was more effective than his life had been; Jesus' life and death combine to save a multitude beyond number from their sins. 3) Samson prayed for God to remember him; Jesus was asked by one of the thieves to remember him when He entered into His kingdom, which He did.*

## Our Mission

🔵 What hope does it give us to see Samson mentioned as a man of faith in Hebrews 11? *If this was the only account of Samson we had in the Bible, then you might wonder if Samson actually believed in the Lord. But guess who shows up in Hebrews chapter 11? Samson. (See Heb. 11:32-34.) Along with Abraham, Isaac, Jacob, and David is the name of Samson, who walked by faith in God. Though it took Samson years for God to strip him of his pride, eventually this giant of a man was clothed in God's mercy, which is a hopeful reality for us.*

✋ Why shouldn't we live a "minimalist Christianity," which is essentially the mind-set that asks of us only the bare amount one can do and still be a Christian? *While Samson had made a Nazirite vow with his mouth, the vow never made it into his heart. Perhaps as a boy he walked in the faith of his parents, but by the time he was an adult, his true colors showed. Samson's flirtation with sin is a lesson for us. As Christians, we should not ask, "How far can I go?" or "How close can I get to the world without sinning?" The real question we should ask instead is: "How can we be holy as an expression of love for Jesus?"*

## Pray

Close your group in prayer, expressing your trust that God will shine through your weakness to make Himself and His kingdom known.

# GOD WAS FAITHFUL TO PROVIDE KINGS, BUT...

As Israel settled into the promised land, they learn that even the best kings still fall short of God's commands. The people demanded a king, and God provided, but they would soon realize their need for a greater King to come.

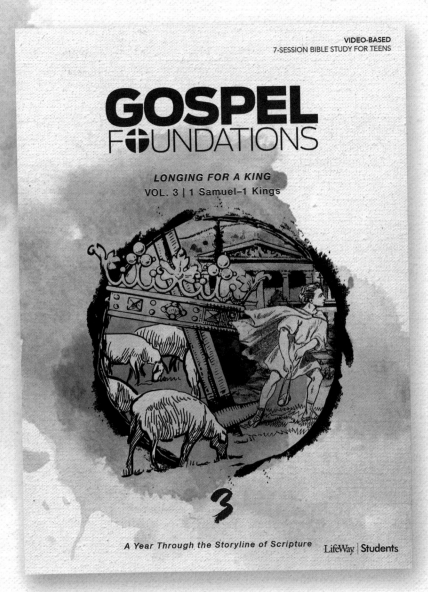